WHY SHE STAYED?

The decisions we make in life, can change everything.

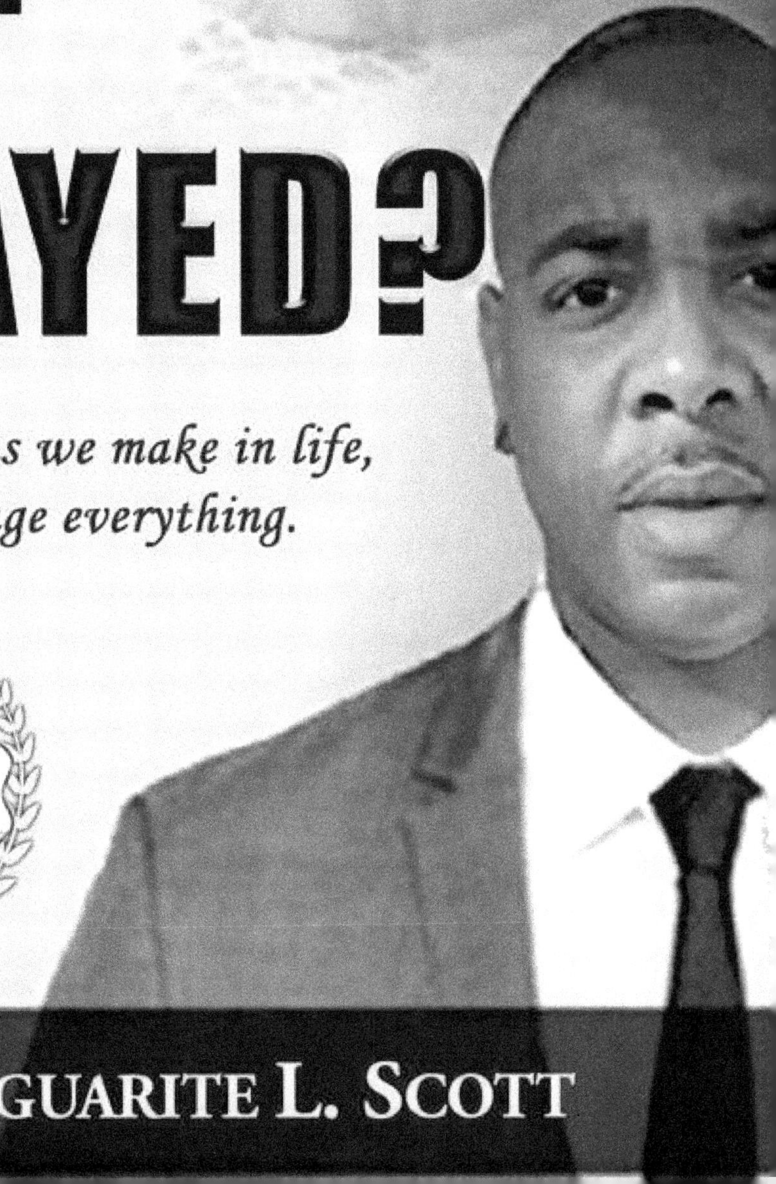

MARGUARITE L. SCOTT

Copyright @2023 by Marguarite L. Scott

All rights reserved. No part of this book may be reproduced in any form or by any electronic or mechanical means, including information storage and retrieval systems, without permission in writing from the publisher, except by reviewers, who may quote brief passages in a review.

This publication contains the opinions and ideas of its author. It is intended to provide helpful and informative material on the subjects addressed in the publication. The author and publisher specifically disclaim all responsibility for any liability, loss or risk, personal or otherwise, which is incurred as a consequence, directly or indirectly, of the use and application of any of the contents of this book.

WORKBOOK PRESS LLC

187 E Warm Springs Rd,

Suite B285, Las Vegas, NV 89119, USA

Website: https://workbookpress.com/
Hotline: 1-888-818-4856
Email: admin@workbookpress.com

Ordering Information:

Quantity sales. Special discounts are available on quantity purchases by corporations, associations, and others.

For details, contact the publisher at the address above.

Library of Congress Control Number:

ISBN-13: 978-1-960752-59-8 (Paperback Version)

978-1-960752-60-4 (Digital Version)

REV. DATE: 02/21/2023

Why She Stayed?

The decisions we make in life can change everything.

By Marquarite L Scott

TABLE OF CONTENTS

ACKNOWLEDGEMENT 1

FOREWARD 2

CHAPTER 1: New Beginning 4
    I had a dream.
    God Shows me my husband.
    Longing for my earthly father.
    Falling in love for the first time. My first love encounter.
    Making bad mistakes.
    Falling in love with my friendly.
    An Annulment

CHAPTER 2: Marriage 38
    Being a wife, she must please, her Husband.
    Helping family

CHAPTER 3: The Moment I Stop Breathing 45
    First time God audibly speaks to me. I finally get my answer.

CHAPTER 4: Going Through the Hurt 69
    Back Together Again. At Home Bible Study.
    A marriage money challenge.
    What is done in dark will come to light. My house was broken in.
    Will I ever get a break?

CHAPTER 5: God Answer Prayers 110
My return will never be the same.

CHAPTER 6: My Child Was Born 123
April 2008 A beginning. Now is the time to walk in my calling. Prophet Sean Mychael Death of a close friend. Time for me to preach. Hope for a new home.

CHAPTER 7: I Had Enough 146
19th Anniversary Marriage and Changes My finial dreams Prophet Sean Mychael had a vision. Peace of God Unconditional Love

Acknowledgment

I thank my Heavenly Father for giving me wisdom, understanding, and teaching me how to love unconditionally.

Thank you Lucinda Louis (Diane) for being an awesome friend and a true Woman of God. Your input throughout this assignment was impeccable. Diane has been a great friend. Her wisdom and relationship with God were truly appreciated.

Thank you, Diane, for helping me from the beginning to the end. I love you so much! A special thanks to Peter Ross, Jr. for loving me forever and always!

I also would like to thank Hazel Lewis Thomas, Randy Lewis, Fredrick Lewis, Carla Lewis, and Kimberly L. Dixon, my good friends, Taura Pritchett and Karen Green, for their support. Thanks to a very special teacher and friend Winifred O'Neal.

Thanks to the creative design by INSIGHTS, LLC in Care of: Silvette Ennis-Holmes.

Also, a special thanks to my friend Editor Rachel Faulker.

INTRODUCTION

In 2005, God told me to write a book. I said, "God, do You know who I am?" I don't consider myself a writer. I love math, science and mostly formulas. I didn't walk across the graduation stage in high school because of my last English test grade which was an "F". I had to take an English class that summer at a university, and I passed. Go figure! I couldn't pass my English test in high school, but I was able to go to a university, pass the test, graduate high school, and go to college. Why did God allow this to happen? Now, I am writing this book about what He wants me to write. God always has a reason for what He is doing. He always knows the outcome and what is going to happen. God uses our past mistakes to teach us how He will use us for His perfect plan. I have problems with English. Therefore, God gets all the Glory for writing this book, not me. I have learned in my life, it's not about me. It's always about Him and His way, which is always good.

When I was about seven years old, I was seeking love, not knowing what love was or what it can do. I wanted love. At that age, love sounded like something good. I always listened to the radio, and heard about love through songs. The radio was my "love teacher". The love songs made me desire that kind of love, which I know now, the difference of love. By listening to the love songs, I learned there is good, bad, happy, and sad love. The words to a song called "I Got Love on My Mind" made me want love even more. In the late 70's, there was a show that had black artists come to perform their music. The lady that sings "I

Got Love on My Mind" was one of the artists on the 70's show. This was the first time I saw her perform. There were mostly black commercials during the airing of this show. She was one of the representatives for a black hair product commercial. She had beautiful hair, and she was perfect for that commercial. She had love, beauty, and style. I wanted that kind of love, look, and style.

What I learned in my life is that love is a Him, and this Him can't be explained to a natural eye. Only a spiritual eye can see it. It took me twenty years to learn this. The love I knew was not the love I needed to get me to the place I was going.

Learning from a spiritual place taught me that. The love I wanted so badly, I always had. Growing in Him showed me who Love is. Today, I am in a place where unconditional love is the greatest of all.

June, 1985, I was sixteen years old. I met my first love. As I grew into a woman, at the age of forty, I realized I was closer to where I need to be with Him. I learned the greatest love will happen when you ask Him to come into your life. Remember, good or bad, God is always teaching us something to grow closer to Him. Here's my story.

Chapter 1
A New Beginning

In November of 1993, my brother Evan asked me to attend the church where he fellowshipped. It was a non-denomination church. I had never been to this kind of church. I was born a Baptist. The Baptist Church I attended the choir's songs were so long. The songs didn't interest me, and I didn't want to hear them. My main purpose when I attended church was to continuously be saved because I felt guilty of something that I did the previous week. I told Evan I would go to church with him. That Sunday morning was the greatest change in my life. I walked in the church, and they were singing a song. It was the sweetest sound I've ever heard in a church. I really listened to the words of that song.

There were white and black people at this church serving God on one accord. I loved it! The pastor began to pray before he preached. I listened to every word of his prayer. The beginning and the end of his prayer stayed with me. At the beginning, he said, "Lord, I repent for sins known and unknown", and he completed his prayer with "In Jesus Name". He began preaching with the title of his message, "We Should Always Repent", then he explained repentance. He said," Pray and ask God to forgive you for what you've done. Turn away from that sin. Change your heart and mind". I thought I was just coming to church to get saved. No one ever told me all I had to do was repent when I sin. In reality, we just have to let God know we are sorry for doing the sin. Now I know God forgives me. I don't have to get saved every time I go to church.

This church was what I needed to get an understanding of God and His Word. I started going there every Sunday. The doors were opened every time I was there. This church had cell group meetings in the neighborhoods all over Baton Rouge. I began going to cell group meetings with Evan. They helped me learn more about the Bible. I wanted and needed to be there. Before I attended these meetings, no one ever told me I'm blessed in the city and in the field. The cell group helped me understand scriptures. I found out God's name is "Love". I was looking for "Love" in all the wrong places.

I always had God's love. No one ever told me I was loved this way. My grandmother taught Evan and I about God. She taught us what she knew.

She'd make me read the Bible to her, but she didn't give me an understanding of the Word. This God kind of love was better than anything I could ever imagine. I needed this God, all day, every day. I got saved for the last time. In the cell group, I learned the Trinity: Father, Son and Holy Spirit. I was taught I have the Holy Spirit living inside of me. Evidence is speaking in tongues which is another language only God can understand. I wanted to speak God's language that night. The Holy Spirit is our teacher and advocate, and I wanted Him. They prayed for me to receive Him. I didn't speak in tongues that night. The group leader said, "You already have Him. He just hasn't manifested Himself yet". I kept praying and reading the Bible. I began reading the Bible more and more. I needed everything God had for me.

I Had a Dream

Joseph had a dream, and when he told it to his brothers, they hated him more. Gen. 37:5

Having a dream and telling someone about your dream is not always a good thing. So, why tell anyone? God has a way to show His work through a dream. It helps our faith, so tell it.

Months passed, and Evan didn't need my help anymore. I moved out of Evan's house and rented an apartment. I always felt I had to stay busy. I was going to school, working at a department store part time, and an automotive shop part time as well. I began exercising, and I continued studying the Word of God. I was very lonely. I had given up the sin of sleeping with every man I met. I was spending a lot more time on my own. I asked God to show me my husband. Days later, God gave me a dream. There were two men sitting on a sofa.

One of the men was a gorgeous man. I knew one, TC, but the other man I had never seen before. I remembered as a little girl, around twelve years old, there was a woman at a park where I had gone to visit with my family. I didn't know her. She walked up to me and said, "You're going to have a dream about two men. Don't pick the man you want". When I woke up, I heard the woman saying that to me as if she was right there. At this time, I was twenty-four years old. It was amazing how the lady that told me not to choose the one I wanted, that dream came to pass that day.

I've been engaged twice. Once, at the age of sixteen, with a guy, at the time, I thought was my first love named Johnny, and second, with a guy that I only loved his personality. It had nothing to do with love or money. The last guy I was engaged to would often come to the department store with one of his friends. We broke up before I moved in with Evan, but I was still wearing his engagement ring. It was a two-carat diamond ring. I loved it so much that I couldn't take it off. He didn't have a car, which was one of the reasons I broke up with him. He was able to take care of me financially, but he had no future goals.

Once I arrived at the department store, my ex- fiancé was standing outside with his friend. He said, "Let's talk". I said, "You're going to make me late for work". He said, "I was looking for you at

Evan's house. I didn't know you moved out. Where do you live now?". I said, "I'll call you later", then walked in the store. The customer service girl said to me, "Hey girl, we have a new guy...". I quickly said, "No!". She said, "He's so cute". I just walked away. On my way clocking in, I heard the assistant manager talking about the new guy with another co-worker. She spoke highly of him. She said she worked with him before. I heard her say, "He's funny and cute". I clocked in and began working. I didn't personally meet him that day.

My friend and co-worker, Octavia, called me that night to ask me if I met Chase. I said, "No, but it seems like he's got to be something very special because everyone at the store can't stop talking about him". She said, "He's funny like you". I said, "Girl, that's crazy. You know I'm stupid. They're making him a star. I'm not a star. I can joke around a little bit, but so can you".

She said, "Girl, you're going to like him". I said, "Ok, we'll see". A couple of days later at work, I saw him from a distance.

He was joking around with someone. I thought, "He's going to play around like a kid. I don't care how cute they think he is. If he's lazy, I don't want to work with him". Bill, a co-worker, walked up to me with Chase, and introduced him to me. He said, "This is Chase. He's going to be working with us stocking". Chase said something to me I thought was stupid. I said, "Boy, I'll stab you". Bill said, "Man, she's just tripping. She plays around just like you". As they walked away, I heard Chase say, "She wanted to stab me. It's going to be a stabbing fest in this store! Who does she think she is?". Bill said, "Come on, let me show you what we're going to be doing".

As I walked to the front of the store, the girl at the service desk asked me if I met her boo, Chase. I said, "Girl, you can do much better than that".

Chase was manipulating everyone into thinking he's the man. He would joke his way in and out of anything. I said, "Girl, you're not going to go far with him. Let him go. Don't just walk, run away!".

Chase had the older women falling all over him, especially Ms. Pam. I heard the women in a group talking about Chase. They said, "Chase could get any woman in here". I said, "Nope, he can't get me".

I was working in the toy department while Chase and Bill worked in the hardware department. When stock was completed in any department, you had to help other departments. The hardware department was closest to where I worked, so I would help in that department most of the time. This gave me the opportunity to get to know Chase better. He was not as bad as I thought. He actually was okay.

Chase and I began talking as co-workers. Chase was joking about something no one else had seen, except me. We laughed, and hit it off from there. We started working together more often.

Octavia was ordering the merchandise for the store. She came by us to check out why so much laughter was going on. She called me aside, and asked what I thought about Chase. I said, "He's alright". Chase and I had a moment of laughter, then I said, "I think he's a good worker. At first, I didn't think he would work at all because of his joking and playing around, but he's okay". Our jokes were always on the same page. We started joking so much, and no one else understood what we were joking about. We worked good together, and got the stocking done faster.

About a month later, the store wanted everyone who stocked to work full-time which also increased our wages. We worked from 10pm to 6am. I worked these hours before, so it wasn't a big deal for me. I wanted Octavia and Bill to work with us, but neither could do it because she had children, and Bill was in high school. Chase, Ms. Pam, other employees and myself started working the night shift. Chase and I grew closer as we worked together. Chase helped me once he finished working in his department. During this time, we began talking about personal things.

God, Show Me My Husband

If any of you lack wisdom, you should ask God who gives generously to all without finding fault, and it will be given to you. James 1:5

One morning, while we were clocking out, Chase asked me to bring him home. His cousin had his car. I said, "Okay, I'll take you home". As we walked out, Chase noticed I needed air in my front tire. As we were driving, Chase said, "Pull over there", as he pointed at a gas station, "I'll put air in your tire". When we got there, he got out of the car to put air. When he stood up, I noticed he was the other man in my dream God gave me months ago. I was in awe, maybe shocked! Chase got back in the car. He looked at me and asked, "What's wrong?". I said, "Nothing". I didn't say a word on the drive to his house. As he got out of the car, he said, "I hope everything's okay with us. You didn't say anything on the way back". I said, "You and I are great. I have no problem with us". He said, "You had me worried". I spoke. "Don't be. See you later at work tonight". I made it home and went for my usual walk. I was thinking so hard about what I saw at the gas station, that I started running. As I ran, I thought, "He's not my type. He doesn't look like the men I would date. He's immature, and he works at a department store. I want a grown-up man that has a real good job. Lord, you know I need someone more responsible who, and who cares about someone other than himself". However, as I grew closer to Chase, I saw another side of him. He was compassionate, charming, witty, smart, handsome and had potential for greatness. I thought, "I think it just might work. I know God knows what He's doing". After that long walk and all the running, I was tired. I never spent over two hours exercising. I got home, took a bath, and fell asleep. I slept nine hours! It was time to eat and get ready for work.

The next day, I went to work. It was business as usual. Chase and I began talking, but I didn't let him know that he was the "One". It wasn't time to tell him about my dream of him being my husband. Chase said he was going to Kansas to meet his wife's family. I said, "Wait a minute, you're married?". He said, "Yes. I got married in February". I was shocked because he flirted with every woman around. I thought, "How can he be in a new marriage and do what he does?". I said to him, "You don't wear a ring". He said, "I don't need to". He never met her family, and was leaving that weekend to meet his in-laws. I asked him about his marriage. He said they got married on the Naval Base. The marriage was for the money. She was an officer in the Navy. He said, "We can get more money if we're married". I didn't know if that was true or not, but I believed him. "Now, I need to meet her family", he said. I asked him if he was going alone. He said, "Yes, and I'm not scared".

We laughed because we both knew he was scared to go alone. He asked me to take him to New Orleans airport, which I did. On the ride back, I started thinking, "This can't be my husband. He's married, and has children. Okay, maybe it's because God knows I can't have children, so He's going to give me a man with children already.

Maybe, Chase is getting a divorce. No, he never said he was getting a divorce".

I went to Evan's house. I noticed his girlfriend had moved in. The kids loved her. Evan was in the process of getting a divorce from his wife. It seemed like he was happy. Evan told me several of my ex-fiancés had been calling. Evan said, "You should give them your number". I said, "I'm trying to get my head straight with God. I don't have time for them right now. I just came here to see if you needed any help. I'm leaving now, so call me if you need me".

I needed groceries, so I went to the store. While shopping, I saw my old friend Karen. We started talking. She told me she moved in another house and asked me to come by. I said, "Okay. When we're finished shopping, I can follow you home". When we got to her house, she showed me around. We got something to drink and sat in her living room. We began talking about what was going on in our lives. Karen asked me if I was dating. I said, "Yes, kind of". I started talking about Chase and the affect he had on me. I told her Chase was in Kansas at this time with his wife. I said, "Yes, he's married". She was in awe because it always seemed to her like I had my life together. She knew I wanted a baby and a happy family. I had to get married to have that, but not like this. I said, "I know it's complicated, but I know in time he'll be mine. Karen, I'm in love with him like I was in love with Johnny, but stronger. Enough about me. I ask her. What's going on with you and your guy?

Are you happy?". She said, "Yes, and he comes with benefits". I said, "That's wonderful. Are you thinking about marriage?". She said, "Marriage has always been something I thought about. I don't know at this time". Changing the subject, Karen said she wanted to get another tattoo. She asked me to go with her. I said, "Right now?". She said, "Yes". So, I followed her to go get her another tattoo. When we got there, Karen told me to pick out one, and she'd pay for it. Karen always paid for things for me. This time, maybe it was her way of apologizing for the past, or she was just being a good friend. As I looked for a tattoo I liked, Chase was on my mind. I wondered if everything in Kansas was going okay, and if he was really going there to get an annulment. I chose a drawing of an angel holding a harp over the word "Love". I really didn't want a tattoo, but the word "Love" made it all good. We got our tattoos. As we left, Karen said, "Call me when Chase gets back, and I'll come over to see your place and meet him". I said,

"Okay, I sure will".

Days later, I went to the airport to pick up Chase. I asked him how was his trip. He said, "It was okay, but not the same". I started talking about his marriage. He said he liked it the way it was before they parted. I said, "Well, we have forty-five minutes before we get home, which means we have lots of time to talk about it". Chase continued talking about his wife. He said, "Maybe, it's the long-distance relationship". I asked him if he loved her. He said, "I was never in love with her because the marriage was an arrangement". He asked me if I loved Rock. I said, "I do love him, but it's not like the love I'd have for my husband". I think at that time in my life, I just wanted someone to want me. I really wanted what I had with Johnny. Chase asked about Johnny, so I told him our story. Chase said, "I feel sorry for your husband for having to fill the giant void. Do you think you'd ever take him back?". I said, "I'm saved now. I'm in a different place. I just want to be with who God wants me be with. My love for Johnny will never go away. I feel if you really love someone, you'll always love them. Yes, I'll always love him, but I know the love I'll have for my husband will be greater".

Chase said, "You are saved. That's good. All my life, my mother, my grandmother, and my grandfather told me I'd be a pastor. Every school I attended was a Christian school. I graduated from a Christian school called Bethany High School. I said, "That's the church where I finally got saved! I'm attending that church right now. Chase, I can see you as a pastor. When I first met you, I thought you were a crazy fool". He said, "I tricked you". I said, "Yes, you sure did. I believe you are greater than you think you are". Chase asked me, "You think so?". I said, "I know so". We finally made it to his house. He went to hand me money. I said, "Thank you, but you don't have to pay me. I'm not in need of your money". He said, "Thank you, for more reasons than one. I said, "Okay, I got to go on that note. I'll see you tomorrow".

The next day, we continued talking about the calling God had on his life, and his family. He asked me if I had any children. I said, "No". "Why do you have those car seats in the back of your car?", he asked. I answered, "Those are for my niece and nephew, my brother's children. I pick them up from daycare Monday through Friday. I help him when he needs me. His wife left him and the kids". I felt I had to explain to him why my brother needed my help. "Evan was married to his wife with two children. He was working at the time, and still working today, at a plant. His wife picked out a house to buy, and Evan bought it. It was a nice beginner's home. Evan called me about 11:00pm from out of town in California one night. He said, "My wife left my children in the house alone". I rushed over to Evan's house. We always entered through the door to the kitchen which was in the back of the house. The kitchen door was open and the lights were on. I walked to the kid's room. My niece was awake, but my nephew was sleeping. It seemed he cried himself to sleep. They smelled bad, and their diapers were soaked. I cleaned baby girl and fed her. Then, I woke baby boy up, cleaned, and fed him too. I called Evan to let him know what I had seen. It hurt my heart to see anyone mistreating babies that way. I let Evan know that I'd stay with the kids until he came home. Evan was gone about a week. When he got back, I moved in because he needed my help. I was working part time at a department store, and part time at an automotive shop. I took the kids to daycare. I let the daycare know I was their aunt, and the one taking care of them until my brother returned from California".

Longing for My Earthy Father

Chase asked if I had any other brothers. I said, "I have two brothers and two sisters. We lived with my mother, Vera". "What about your dad?", he asked. I said, "I met him about two years ago. It was the best thing that happened to me". When I was a little girl, I wanted to know my dad. I wanted him to take me on a picnic so we could sit for hours and talk, but my mother didn't want me to meet him. She would say, "Why you want to see that broken-down man? He didn't want you". I longed for my father to love me. She told me I'd never meet him. I wanted to meet my daddy so bad.

At twenty-two years old, I still wanted to meet my father. I called my Aunt Debra, and asked her if she knew my dad. She said, "Yes". I asked her where he lived. She said, "Dutchtown. Go there, and ask for Plunkum at any gas station or store". "Plunkum?", I asked. "Yes, ask anyone there.", she said. The next weekend, I went to Dutchtown. I stopped at a side store, and asked if anyone knew Plunkum. A guy said, "Yes, that's my uncle. Would you like me to take you to him?". "Yes", I replied. He got in my car. I was so nervous. I was finally going to meet my dad! I drove about two miles from the store, turned a corner, and two houses down there he was sitting under the carport. When I got out the car to meet him, he knew exactly who

I was before I told him my name. He said, "Look at my daughter, Faith". I was shocked he knew my name and that I was his daughter. There were many people around his house. He said to them, "Come meet my daughter". He introduced me to his wife. I had a cousin that lived on the same street. He called him to come meet me. I was so happy to finally meet my dad. I could hardly breath. It finally happened! The man that I wanted all my life was right in front of me. We talked about things in my life. It was getting late, so I told him I had to go. He asked me to come back the next weekend so we could have a picnic. I was about to cry because that was all I wanted from him. I told him it would be an honor for me to come back and have a picnic with my father.

I went to Vera's house to tell my sisters I finally met my dad. Vera heard us talking. She asked, "You met that broken-down man?". I said, "Vera, he knew who I was. He called me by my name before I could say it. We're going to have a picnic on Saturday. I don't know how he knew I wanted him to take me on a picnic. I dreamed my dad would take me on a picnic". Vera walked away. I didn't care what she thought about it. I saw my dad! It was my dream come true! I don't think I had ever been happier.

Saturday couldn't come fast enough. At last, it was Saturday, and I was at my dad's house asking him questions about his family. I asked, "Didn't you ever want to see me?". He answered, "Yes, I wanted to see you. Your mama did not want me to see you. Your mama and me were messing around while I was married. She got pregnant, and wanted me to leave my wife. I told her I wasn't going to leave my wife, but I would take care of my child. She didn't want it that way. So, she told me I'd never see you. When she moved to Baton Rouge, I found out where you stayed, but she moved so much. Every time I would find you, you were gone again". I said, "Yes, we did move a lot. Every time she didn't pay the rent, we had to move. I'm sorry

I didn't spend time with you. Vera told me you didn't want me. For a little while, I believed her. When I saw you, and you knew who I was, it erased all the wrong. Thank you for this. I always wanted to have a picnic with my father". We were there for hours. A lot was said, and we both got what we needed that day.

I asked Chase if he had any brothers and sisters. He responded, "No, I'm an only child. I have two cousins who are like brothers to me. We grew up together. We were always with my grandmother and grandfather". I said, "My grandmother and grandfather were like my parents, also. We called my grandmother "Madea", and Mr. John L. Boyd was my grandfather. Madea taught me how to cook. One time, I was frying a chicken that I had to go in the backyard to kill first. After I murdered that chicken and cooked it, I couldn't eat it. All I could see was its eyes. It said, "Please don't eat me". I just couldn't eat it. She also taught me how to sew using a pattern at a young age. She always made me read the Bible to her. I was about six or seven at the time. I still don't know how I learned to read the King James Bible. It's such a hard book to read. She told me I'd be a minister someday. I wondered if God knew I cussed. If so, why would He pick me? Madea told me she'd have Godly visions about me. I believed I would be a minister, but I just didn't want it. I had to make me some money. I thought pastors didn't make big money unless people pay tithes, and I knew I didn't pay them at the time. I'm tithing to my church now. I know that was selfish of me at the time. I figured if I tithed, others would too". He said, "You have leadership all over you. Are you a prophetess?". I said, "No! Madea said I would be a minister, so don't add more to it". I thought in my mind, "I know God had a plan for us. I just can't tell him yet".

Falling in Love for the First Time

At seven, I didn't know what love was, but I knew it was a good thing. When I got saved with the love of God, I learned a little more about love. Love is something I always had. This Love is called Jesus. No one can love me more than Him.

But I have this against you, that you have abandoned the love you had at first. Rev. 2:4

Chase said, "Tell me more about your relationship with Johnny". I started off saying, "Well, Johnny was my first love, and it had a great impact on my life. I was sixteen at the time I met him. My cousin Kenny would come over to our house from time to time, and we'd go for a ride sometimes. He'd say, "I got somebody I want you to meet". I said, "Where is he?". Kenny would always say, "I'm going to bring him over". June 20,1985, Kenny finally brought his friend over. I met Johnny J Ross This friend was very handsome, gorgeous, and "a pretty boy". He was not pretty, but beautiful to me. He looked like a singer. I instantly fell in love with him. He asked me if I'd like to go to the movies with him. I said, "Yes". I went in the house to ask Vera if I could go. She said, "No, you just met this boy". I told her Kenny was going with us. Again, she answered, "No". I went out to tell him, then we exchanged phone numbers. That was the beginning of a new friendship.

Johnny called me as soon as he got home. He was now "officially" my boyfriend. He was eighteen, and his birthday was August 19th. He graduated from Capitol High School, and would be attending college in the fall. Johnny lived with his mother.

We spent the whole summer teaching each other love. We both needed someone to love, and someone who would appreciate love, not take that love for granted. He understood what love meant.

Love is not something, it is Someone. We appreciated being together, not just using each other for stuff or money. At a young age, I loved this song "I Got Love on My Mind". In the song, it said "love was like laughing in the rain". I remember running outside as a little girl in the rain singing that song. Madea would cry out, "Come in this house before you get a "hook worm". She asked what I was doing. I told her I was trying to get some love from the rain. I still don't know what's a "hook worm". Later we had a talk, and she tried to explain love to me, she said, "Love is a feeling you feel for someone special. You'll know because you won't feel like that for anybody else.

It's hard to explain to you now, but you'll know". Now, I know nothing feels greater than love.

We spent so much time together learning daily about love. I told him what Madea said about love. He said no one ever explained love to him. I think he thought I had another boyfriend before Johnny. I said Although, there was this one guy. I liked him a lot. He was my cousin Lee friend, and he was handsome. I thought he was going to be the one, but he was doing drugs. I told Johnny about him, and we didn't talk about him anymore. Johnny told me there was a girl he thought he loved. Her name was Dina. I saw her, and she was very pretty. I felt a little intimidated, but he assured me that she'd never be me. He also told me he had a baby boy.

The baby was about three months old when I met him. I loved him anyway. He could've had lots of children, that didn't matter.

Love is learning to accept people for who they are no matter the good, the bad, or the ugly. It's all part of growing up. Everyone has things they need to change. We should be willing to change the bad to good at some point in our lives. Growing up should be changing up. I was changing. We were destined to be together. Johnny would sing to me. He didn't just look like a gorgeous singer he sounded like one too. That's when I learned I could sing. We would sing together as we listened to music. Hip Hop love songs were so beautiful in the 80's. The words were meaningful and true. I think the song "Are You the Woman" was one of our favorite songs. These love songs tell a story about the singer's love for someone. Johnny and I could relate to every word. We both were looking for love.

Johnny talked about his dad. He was a big-time drug dealer. He owned a social club that had an apartment at the top of the building. His dad was building a townhouse next door to the club. He said Johnny could move in the apartment above the club. Johnny rode his bicycle to my house every day that summer. We did so many things together. We went to the movies with my brother Evan and his girl-friend. We walked downtown, and had a picnic in the park. It didn't matter where we went, as I long as I was with Johnny. Johnny talked about how much he liked to paint. At the time, I wanted to work in a hospital as a manager of some kind. I didn't know what, but anything in a hospital. I always liked taking care of people. We talked about how many kids we wanted (two boys, one girl), and how our house would look (three bedrooms, two bathrooms, den, big kitchen, because he liked to cook and so did I, and a two- car garage with a white picket fence). Johnny has two brothers and one sister. One brother was in jail, and the other was in college. His sister lived in California. Johnny wasn't close to his brothers or his sister, but I was very close to my sisters and brothers. Johnny wanted our family to be close, loving, unselfish and sharing, just to name a few things. We vowed to always teach them how to love. A loving family was so important to us. It was something we both needed".

My First Love Encounter!

"Once summer was over, I started at Capitol High School, and Johnny began his sophomore year in college. I was working at a fast-food restaurant.

Johnny started working different jobs. His dad finished building his townhouse, so Johnny moved in the apartment above the club. Johnny's dad bought him a car. He would pick me up and take me to work. He taught me how to drive his car. It was a manual stick shift. We talked about intercourse. Johnny said he didn't want to have it until I was ready. We'd kiss and touch, but no intercourse. Johnny was in college, but he never made me feel he wanted any girl from college. He was always with me everywhere I went. I didn't want to be without him. Sometimes when we went on a date, my step-dad would be near, checking to see if we were where we should be.

It was almost two years we were together. I was about to turn eighteen, and this was the year. I set in my mind to make love at eighteen. My grandmother taught me about how intercourse before marriage was a sin. She didn't teach me how to control those urges I had. It's April 27th, and I tell Johnny it is time for us to do it. Johnny said, "Are you sure?". "Yes, tomorrow is my 18th birthday", I said. On my birthday, Johnny took me out to dinner. Afterward, we went to his apartment. He prepared his apartment with candles, red roses, red wine, and baby blue satin sheets on the bed. He had my favorite music playing with my favorite incense smell. Johnny asked me, "Are you sure you want to do this?". I said, "Yes!". Johnny made love to me. It was awesome, fabulous, incredible, and magnificent. I was in the greatest place ever. I didn't know why it took me so long, but it was worth the wait. The bad things my friends warned me about would happen, didn't happen at all. I was now at another level in life.

About two months later, I began sleeping a lot, and throwing up. Johnny said I was pregnant. We went to the doctor to get checked. I was pregnant! We went back to the apartment to talk about what we were going to do. We both wanted to keep the baby. Johnny said he would quit school, and get another job while I finished high school. We could stay at the apartment until we found another place to live. It seemed we had a good plan. Johnny had to go downstairs to do something for his dad. He noticed my step-dad's car outside in the parking lot. He came back upstairs to tell me. I turned off the light so I could look down out the window. I saw my step-dad pulling out of the parking lot.

Johnny said, "Let me take you home". As we were pulling up to my house, my step-dad and Vera were in the front yard with the porch light on, as if something bad had happened. My step-dad had Evan's shot gun in his hand. When we got out of the car, he pointed the gun at Johnny's chest. Vera looked mad. She told me to go inside the house, so I did. I watched out the window. I heard my step- dad say, "You took her upstairs to have intercourse with her". I felt so scared for Johnny's life. I thought it was all my fault. Johnny argued back saying, "That's not true". I could see the fear in his eyes. Johnny finally got in his car, and drove away.

Vera came in the house. She said, "You can't see him anymore". I told Vera, Johnny was not that kind of person. She yelled, "He can get you pregnant!". I wanted to tell her I was pregnant already, but I couldn't do that after what I saw that night. I went to my room. I thought the rest of the night about our baby, and how Johnny was misunderstood by Vera. It was my choice to make love, not his. I thought I could move in with Johnny. I would drop out of school, and get a job. Johnny called me about 2:00am that morning. He asked, "How long has your step-dad been trying to sleep with you? Did you have intercourse with him?". I told him no, but that he would always touch and feel on the private parts of my body. A couple of times he scared me by watching me take a bath. Johnny said, "I knew it!". I asked him how he knew. "It was the way he acted tonight. It's like you are his prized possession", he said. Johnny told me to get some sleep, and he would call me later to pick me up somewhere. Finally, I went to sleep.

The next day, Johnny picked me up. I told him that I loved him so much, and I'd rather not have the baby. I wanted him more than this baby. Johnny said, "I want you and this baby too. I'm not worried about your step-dad". We talked for days on how much we wanted that baby, how the baby would make a big difference in our lives, and how it would be nice to come home to a real family.

After all our thoughts, we decided not to have the baby. A week passed. We went to get an abortion.

The abortion reminded me of a terrible death, like the loss of my grandmother. Johnny cried because he wanted us to start our family. He grew up always wanting a family of his own. We started preparing for another baby by saving money, and looking for another place to stay. Johnny told me he was thinking about why we had an abortion. "Was it because your step-dad put the gun to my chest?", he asked. Johnny was distraught about this, among other things that happened in his past. He turned to drugs. His dad had cocaine in the club, and Johnny tried it for the first time. Since then, he has been on drugs.

The next year, Johnny was still in college and working odd jobs, but things started to change. He had a new group of friends. Johnny started smoking marijuana. In the beginning, it was okay. Then he started smoking it every day. He was cooking marijuana in the oven at the apartment, and selling drugs out of his dad's club. It was out of control. Things were changing between us. A week before prom, Johnny and I went to his mama's house. I asked him what was going on between us. He was high on cocaine, and I was talking to him about how high he was. He got angry, and hit me so hard, then pushed me out of the patio glass door. Once I got up, I called my cousin, Kenny, to come get me. I told him what happened. He picked me up, then took me to his house. I broke up with Johnny that night. We didn't go to the prom together. The week of prom, I was the winner of a free limousine ride. I won a ride, but no date. I asked one of my classmates to go, and he accepted. Nothing was ever the same between me and Johnny after that. I still love Johnny more than life, but Johnny became someone else, and so did I".

Making Bad Mistakes

No matter what you do, God will always be there. I thank God for His goodness and mercy He has for me. Surely your goodness and love will follow me all the days of my life. Psalm 23:6

"I started to hang out with a girl I worked with at a fast-food restaurant. Johnny didn't like her. He said she would get me in a lot of trouble. He wasn't lying. I started stealing out of the cash register at work. I would go to the mall with one of my co-workers. We would steal name brand jeans from clothing stores. I remember folding the jeans so small it would fit in my purse, and I'd walk out the store. There were no shoplifting scanners nor security at the time. She was a student at a university, and said she was pledging. She told me this was part of her initiation. I didn't know if she was lying, nor did I care. I wanted to do it. This was the first time I really thought I was a bad girl. Johnny and I was talking again. We didn't get back together, but we remained friends. Johnny let me use his car, and told me not to wreck it. I went to co-worker's apartment in Johnny's car. When I was getting ready to leave, I saw the car was wrecked. Someone had hit the car while it was parked, then drove off. It was hit so bad. I was surprised because we didn't hear any noise from outside in the apartment. I got in the car, and was so scared to tell Johnny. He told me not to wreck his car and it happened! I went to his apartment to tell him. He was so angry. He said, "I told you not to hang out with that girl". I told him I was not with that girl.

Weeks later, I started stealing again. This time, I was stealing eyeliner and lipstick, and she was stealing pants or name brand clothes. Security caught us, and we went to jail for shoplifting. I called Johnny, and he called his dad. They came bail me out. I told Vera about it, so she called my uncle BoBo. He called his sources to get my name cleared. When I went to court, I had to go to a class to get my record cleared.

Graduation day came, but I didn't walk across the stage. I didn't pass my English class. I went to summer school. I took the ACT test, and made a fifteen. It was good enough to attend a university. I took the ACT test later that year, and made an eighteen which allowed me to attend a better university. I had to prove to myself that I was capable to go to a better university. I applied for summer classes. I was accepted, picked my classes, and began school. I went to school for about six weeks before I realized I needed a full- time job. I finished that semester and began looking for a job.

I needed a car to get back and forth to work. Johnny and I had saved $2785. I took $500 and went looking for a car. I wanted a Mustang. I went to a Ford car lot, and found one. The salesman checked my credit, but I didn't have any. I really wanted that Mustang. They suggested another way to get my credit started. I got a brand- new Ford Festiva with no co-signer, and a $500 down payment. I was working at a fast-food restaurant at this time. I started night classes at a computer school.

I will always love Johnny, but I don't think I would ever get back with him. I still wanted his baby. I began sleeping with men that looked like him, and there were many. They had to look like Johnny for me to sleep with them. I did this for about two years. None of them could get me pregnant. I stopped looking for a man to give me a baby. I realized that it wasn't a baby I wanted. The love I had with Johnny was what I wanted and needed.

One day, I drove to Karen's mother's house to visit Karen. A guy was trying to get my attention. I pulled over to talk to him. He said, "Can I have your number?". I said, "Not right now, but I'm taking applications. Would you like to fill one out?". He started laughing. I said, "I'll take your number, and put it on file. As soon as there's an opening, I'll give you a call". I asked him his name. He said, "My name is Rock". He didn't look like Johnny, but I liked him. A couple weeks later, I called Rock. We talked and started going out. I had fun with him. I asked him about his previous girlfriend, and he said he loved her, but she wasn't the one. He asked me about my relationships. I said there was one man that I was in love with.

Rock graduated from the same high school as Johnny. I asked him if he knew Johnny, the wrestler. He said, "Yes, I remember him". Rock ran track at high school. I saw his exhibit of trophies and awards at his house. That was the beginning of a new relationship. He lived with his mama. We became serious after a year and a half. That's when he gave me this", and I showed Chase the two-carat diamond ring. Chase said, "He must have really loved you". I said, "I believe he did, but I don't think I felt the same kind of love for him that I had for Johnny. We moved in together for a very short time, but it didn't work out. I still see him from time to time, but it's nothing serious. It's time to go", I said. Chase said, "To be continued...". I said, "Yes, but tomorrow is your turn to tell your story".

The next morning, I started spending more time with God. I love all music, but gospel music gives me a feeling I can't explain. It's almost like God's directly talking to me. I fell in love with one song called "He Will Never Let You Down". "The race is not given to the swift nor the strong" is some of the words. Another song, "He's Right on Time" says "you got family all around you, but you're so alone. Even your best friend can be found. Jesus will never let you down". This is what I was feeling in my life that day. I felt so lonely as if no one understood my loneliness, but God always comes through for me. I was spending more time in church and cell groups. I kind of felt lost. I knew He would fix it for me, because He always does. I thought to myself, "I think I can sing pretty good when I sing gospel songs. I'm going to just sing here in my apartment for Jesus".

I will always remember the race is not for the swift nor strong but the ones who endure. Eccl 9:11 is going to be my motto for my life while I am on my way to heaven

I told Chase, "Okay, today is your turn to tell your story". Chase said, "Faith, my life story is nowhere near your life story.

There's only one girl that I deeply cared about. She birthed my son. Her name is Marissa. We got together before I went into the Navy. When I got to Virginia, I met my daughter's mother, Connie. I cared about her. She was so pretty. I didn't think she would want me. We got together, but we began having lots of arguments.

She always thought I was cheating". I said, "I would think that too as much as you flirt with every woman that comes in the store". Chase said, "No, you don't understand. I think I loved her. Then there was Alisha, I don't know if that was love because of the feelings I had for Marissa. That's it!". I said, "Oh, I see! You're such a player, you can't have relationships that would mess up your flow". Chase said, "Yeah, you're right. That would mess me up forever". I said, "That's good to know. I'm just glad you had at least one true relationship. How many children do you have?".

Chase said, "I only have two children; a son with Marissa and a daughter with Connie. This is the two women I truly cared about. I asked, "You cared about them, so you had to make a baby with them?". "I had to plant my seed", he said. I asked him how many more seeds he needed to plant.

Chase said, "I can't put a number on it right now. I'm sure there will be more. Faith, I'll talk more tomorrow".

When I got home. I thought to myself, "My grandmother said that I'll be a minister. I never saw a minister not knowing what they want or need to do. I never saw a minister unhappy or in disarray.

I'm that all day, and I'm sure it will still be there tomorrow. When will it end?". My family and friends thought I was so strong. If they just looked a little closer, they'd see it's not strength. I didn't know what it was. I guess you fake it till you make it. I asked God to help me lose weight. One of the co-workers told me I was losing weight. She asked, "What are you doing to lose?". I said, "I asked God to help me". That day, I knew God was answering my prayers. I hadn't shared things with anyone about my husband God showed me. I wondered how long I would have to wait for my husband.

Falling in Love with My Friend

It was my day off, so I went to Vera's house to see my sisters, brother, and my niece Jada. I always had to bring Jada something. I bought her a stuffed toy. I played with her, and we had a good day. On my way home, I passed by Rock's grandmothers' house. He was outside, so I stopped to talk for a minute. As we were talking, Chase drove by. I stopped him and asked him, "What you doing in this area?". He said, "I'm bringing my grandfather's godson a present. What you doing?". I said, "Nothing, just talking to Rock". Chase said, "Oh, your fiancé". I said, "No boy, he's just a friend".

Chase said, "I'm about to go home and get a nap in before I go to work. I'll see you tomorrow". After Chase drove off, I told Rock I was going home.

Chase lived in the same area as Rock's grandmother. As I was driving, I saw Chase going in the same direction as me. He was waving at me to turn on his street. He yelled, "I got something to tell you". When I got there, he was waiting outside. I said, "What do you have to tell me?". He said, "I believe you're going to be my wife". I asked,

"Have you been talking to Jesus?". He said, "Yes", then he kissed me with those big lips. I was shocked, but it was good. We kissed some more and I was in awe. It was not a dirty or nasty bad boy kiss. It was kind of romantic. I liked it, I really liked it. He asked, "What you going to do?". I said, "Go home and watch this movie called "Poetic Justice" starring Janet Jackson and Tupac". He asked, "Can I come watch it with you before I go to work?". I said, "Boy you going to be sleepy tonight". He said, "I slept this morning". I said, "Okay, come on". I was amazed how God showed Chase what he showed me. I didn't have to say a word.

When Chase got to my apartment, he asked me, "What kind of money do you make?". I asked him, "Would you like some red Kool aid?". He said, "As good as this apartment looks, I wouldn't think you drink red Kool Aid". We both laughed. I said, "It's not how much money you make, it's what you do with the money. I can find a sale. All this stuff was on sale, or put on layaway. I was outside playing with my niece earlier. Let me wash up and change". He said, "I'll watch the Sport Center while I wait". When I was done. We started the movie about twenty minutes later. The movie was watching us. We were in the bed making love for about two hours. It was time for him to go to work. He said, "I could call in". I said, "No, go to work". Before he left, he said, "I will be back in the morning". I said, "I'll see you about 6:15am". He said, "No, 6:10am!".

I called the department store, and my friend Octavia answered the phone. She never worked that late. I asked, "Octavia, what are you doing there?". She said, "Front desk girl called in, so I got her late shift. Girl, Chase walked through the door looking like he just got out of somebody's bed". I said, "He probably did". I asked to speak to him. She called him to the phone. He said, "6:00 am can't get here fast enough. I wanted to do that to you when I first met you. You know, when you said you'd stab me. In my mind, I said, please let me stab you tonight! I didn't think I would care for you like this. I think I loved you when I met you". I said, "That's crazy, but I know God has His hands on this relationship. Not the "doing it" part. It's bigger than that. I'll see you in the morning. I'm going to watch this movie we didn't watch". So, I watched the movie and prayed that God forgave me for the "sin" with a married man. It's 6:15am. I get a knock at my door. It's Chase. He came in with breakfast. We talked, then had more bed time. We were off that weekend. We only went out for food. We continued watching movies, among other things. I did go to church that Sunday. We both prayed, and talked about what we did that weekend. He talked about how he felt when he first met me. He couldn't understand the instant feeling of love he had for me. That's never happened to him before. I asked, "Never?". He said, "Never! I knew you had it before when you were telling me about Johnny. I knew you knew what love was, but I didn't. At that time, I wanted to feel that kind of love. I think God gave it to me through you. I really love you".

Weeks passed by, and we continued sleeping together. I was always going back and forth to God, repenting. Repent means turn away, and don't do it again. I kept doing it. We were now four months in this messy relationship. I felt bad about him being married and we were doing what we were doing. I lost a lot of weight. I needed clothes. Chase went to the mall with me to my favorite department store, Lerner's. He got a credit card in his name as a present for me. Then, we went to Express clothing store, and he got me another credit card. I was a little overwhelmed. No one had ever done this for me. He said, "You are going to be my wife. It's just the beginning of what I'm going to get you. That night, I didn't think about God, Jesus or the Holy Spirit. I had to give him a present, so another two hours, it was on. I introduced him to my family; Vera, my brothers and sisters, and my nieces and nephews. He introduced me to his cousin Sonya, and her boyfriend William.

An Annulment

August,1994, Chase said, "I'm going to Kansas to see my wife. We're going to get an annulment. I love you too much to let you go". I took him to the New Orleans airport. He was gone about a week. I was missing him. Chase and his cousin, Sonya, were close. Chase left her phone number if I needed to talk. She knew how to find him. I'd be out of line to call him there. I called her, and asked if she talked to Chase. She said she didn't, so I asked her to call him. I told her he was out of town with his wife. She asked me when would he be coming home. I told her I wasn't sure. She called Chase, and told him, "Faith misses you". He told her to tell me that he missed me so much, and he was in the process of getting an annulment. He told her as soon as they came to an agreement, he would call me. After that call, I left Sonya alone.

On my way home, I realized I was in love with him. It kind of felt stronger than the love I had for Johnny. I knew that this had to be from God because I had never loved anyone else like Johnny, or even close to what I felt for him. This was way more than what I had for Johnny.

Chase finally came back. He told me it would be finished in about thirty days. I said, "Okay, what now?". He said, "You're going to be my wife". I said, "Okay". He said, "It's time for you to meet my family. My mama is having a fish fry at my grandfather's house this weekend. You can meet my grandfather, aunts, and cousins. My uncle may come. He's on drugs, but may be clean on the weekend. I said, "Good".

Saturday was here. I was nervous to meet his mother. Chase and I walked in. Chase said, "This is Faith". I said hello to everybody. Chase's Aunt Renee walks up to me and says, "We hug here", then hugged me. She said, "Chase finally got it right". At the time, I didn't know what she meant.

Chase introduced me to his mother. She looked at me, and her face said to me, "I don't like her". She said, "Hi". I sat at the table while his mother was frying the fish. She barely looked at me. She fixed a plate of food, and almost threw the plate in front of me. Chase was so embarrassed. He took the plate from me. He said, "I'll eat this". I told his mother, "I'm not hungry". By now, I'm feeling very uncomfortable. Chase ate. When we got up, no one was talking to me. Chase said, "Well, we're going to go". When we got in the car, Chase said, "Just give her a little time. She wasn't there when I married Kathy. So, maybe she's still mad at me". I said, "I'm not Kathy". Chase said, "Faith, I'm her only child. She will adjust sooner or later".

About a week later, I brought Chase to meet my dad. On the way, we saw Johnny painting lines in a parking lot. I smiled and waved at him just to let him know I saw him. Chase had never seen him before. I told Chase, "That guy I waved at was Johnny. Chase said, "He's one of those "pretty boys". He looks like that singer. I said, "Yes he does". After I introduced Chase to my dad, we stayed and talked for a while. Chase asked my dad lots of questions about his job. My dad worked at a chemical plant. Chase asked him what was his position, how much money he made, and how long had he been there. My dad was in his fifties at the time. My dad gave Chase details of everything he did at work. We were there until evening. After we left, Chase started to talk about his dad. Chase said he wanted a relationship with my dad. I said, "We can or you can go back whenever you want".

Chase said, "I just might do that".

I saw my prayers were answered. I realized my faith in God was getting stronger. I was growing up to see myself, but who and what am I? I did not know where this was going. I just knew everything was going to be alright.

CHAPTER 2
MARRIAGE

In January, 1995, Chase's annulment was final. I was happy because I knew God wasn't happy with the intercourse part. We were having it every night. Chase and I started repenting, and praying together. Chase said, "I love Jesus like you, so we can't keep doing this". March 17,1995, St. Patrick's Day, we were at to an Irish restaurant to have dinner for St. Patrick's Day. Chase asked me if I wanted an alcoholic beverage. I asked him, "Are you trying to take advantage of me?". He said, "No, but if it works. You just might want one after I ask you this". I said, "What are you going to ask me Big D?". He said, "I love when you call me Big

D. Would you like to marry me?". I said, "What?". He said, "We can go right over there to the mall and get your ring. Yes or no! Tell me now. This offer won't last long. This is a one-time offer... Okay, the mall closes at 9:00pm, it's 7:23pm, so you got a little time". I said, "You mean this is a one-time offer? I don't get another chance?". He said, "Time is ticking". I said, "Let me think for a moment. Now, you mean you want me to have and to hold till death do us part?". He said, "Girl, you want to get married or not?". I asked, "Do you love me?". He said, "Yes, I love you!". I said, "Wait till after I eat". He said, "Faith, quit playing". I said,

"Yes, I will marry you". He said, "Thank you! You better have said yes with all this good loving I've been giving you". We laughed. He said, "Order, so we can go". We went to the mall to get a ring. As we waited for the salesman, we discussed what day we would get married. We agreed soon, very soon. I said, "Next Friday". Chase agreed.

We couldn't wait to get back to the apartment to celebrate. We celebrated our engagement all weekend. Only time we left the apartment was to go eat something. Monday, we called Bill and Octavia to tell them because we needed witnesses on Friday. We didn't tell anyone else because months before, we were telling people we were together. They all said it wasn't going to last, including Bill and Octavia. They thought that because Chase joked and played so much. Since I was so serious-minded about everything, we were not capable to last in a marriage. Bill and Octavia agreed to be our witnesses. March 24,1995 was the day. Chase was sleeping. He had worked the night before. The morning of our wedding day, I had to pick up my shoes I left at Vera's house. On my way back, I saw Johnny painting in a parking lot. I thought, "What are the odds of this?". I turned around and said, "I'm getting married today". He asked, "Do you love him? Does he make you happy?". I said, "Yes. I believe God sent him to me". He said, "You've always talked to God.

Congratulations!". "Thank you, Johnny", I said, as we hugged. He said, "Don't forget to dance". On the way back to my apartment, I thought, "This could be us today", not thinking God planned all this, even that last moment with Johnny for His purpose. I got back and woke up Chase. We both got ready. Bill and Octavia got there, and we all left together. We got married, then afterward, we went to a restaurant to eat and take pictures. Chase was still sleepy, so we went back to the apartment, and Octavia and Bill went back to their jobs. The next morning when we woke up, we laid there for a while talking about our future. Chase said he had to find a way to make more money to get us a house, and he wanted a better car. Chase was working at Depot Store in the day, and the Postal Plant at night. I was working at Chemical Plant. I said, "The only way I'll leave you is if you make a baby with somebody else in this marriage". The devil heard me. I always wanted a family. Chase said, "You'll be able to have us, and our children together in one house. I got enough children for the both of us". When he said that, I didn't know I was in for a rude awakening.

Being A Wife, She Must Please Her Husband

Marriage is a union between a man and woman, and a foundation of a family. God declared "It is not good that man should be alone." He made a helper suitable for the man Gen.2:18

This meant the world to me to honor God in this way.

Marriage was a completion for me. Good and bad, I know God would be with me all the way. For me, marriage was do or die.

Six months later, we needed another car. I went to the credit union through my job to get a new car. I wanted a Honda Prelude. Chase and I went to a Honda dealer to get my Prelude. Chase said I shouldn't get that car because it cost too much. I really wanted that car. I got a Honda Civic. I wanted that Prelude, but because I was married, we made that decision together. Chase was happy. He liked the Civic. Little did I know at the time, he didn't want me to have what I wanted. He wanted me to have what he wanted me to have. I wanted to share my decision making like a wife should.

Chase began looking for a better job. I was still working at the plant, and going to night classes to be an accountant. Chase began changing. I'm thinking it was because I was making more money than him. Madea always told me, "Don't let your husband feel small". So, I asked Chase if he wanted me to quit my job because I love him more than any amount of money. I told him I'd go back to a department store as a cashier. He said, "No, stay at your job". When he said no, I heard, "What you think? I don't want my wife to make more than me", but he said he was going to get another job. He said, "I'm looking into the post office. You know my mama and my Aunt Renee works there". I said, "What do you have to do?". "The post office has a test coming up. I just need to study", he answered. I told him I would help him study. He said, "You can come take the test with me". I said, "Let's study". He said he could get five extra points because he was in the Navy.

I began praying for Chase to get the job, and for God to give me a baby son. Lord, Chase said that Marissa don't take care of his son the way he would like. His hair's not cut; clothes are not clean. I pray that you keep his son in good health. In Jesus' name, I pray. Amen!

We went together to take the test. I was there to support my husband. He said with doubt, "I know I can pass this". I said, "You're going to pass it, in Jesus' name". As we were taking the test, I re- membered him saying, "Faith, I know you're going to pass this test, and what my grandmother said to me about not letting him feel inferior by me. I didn't try to pass. About a week later, we got the results. Chase passed, and I didn't. I was happy for him.

He got the job at the Post Office. It was exactly what he wanted.

Helping Family

My younger sister, Kim, was staying with us at the time. She moved in after someone broke into my mother's house. The only things stolen was all of Kim's name brand things. We thought it was some- one my little brother, Fredrick, knew. Kim was scared to be there alone after the break in. She was a high school senior, and working a part-time job. So, Chase said she could come stay with us. Since

I had a new car, I taught her how to drive my old car to get back and forth to school and work. She was responsible, so I didn't have to worry about her.

Chase's family was Catholic. His mother and aunt started going to a non-denomination church. He wanted to visit it, so we did. We both fell in love with the church, and joined. I was still hanging out with my cell group friends. I told the cell group leader I still couldn't pray in tongues. He said, "You got it. Just keep praying, you will".

Chase's cousin, Sonya, found out we joined a non-denominational church. She asked if I wanted to go New Orleans to see a certain Prophetess. She said that the Prophetess was preaching with a Texas Preacher. I said, "Yes, I'd like to go". I asked if it was okay if I invited my Aunt Carol. She said it was okay, as long as I was driving. I said, "Yes, I'll drive". The three of us went. It was my first time going to a conference. It was awesome. The preacher made an altar call for anyone who wanted to speak in tongues. I ran down to that isle. That was a night I will never forget. I started speaking in tongues. I was excited all the way home that night. I started singing. Sonya said, "I didn't know you could sing". My aunt said, "Me either". I said, "I'm so happy I can speak in tongues. It's not me, blame the Holy Spirit for this beautiful voice".

They laughed, but I was serious. When I got home, I couldn't wait to tell Chase. I told him, but he wasn't excited. He just said, "That's good". I went to the bathroom. I wanted to practice speaking in tongues so I could speak to God, and no one would know what I was talking to God about. I didn't know until the Holy Spirit revealed it to me. I was practicing for weeks. I learned more as I read the Bible. My tongue would change to a different language. It was awesome.

Chase wanted me to meet his son's mother, Marissa. The next day, we went to meet her. Marissa was pregnant, and she also had a little girl. We were all outside talking. I told her that I would like to keep their son sometimes, so he could get to know me. Before we left, Marissa pulled me to the side and said, "I would like you to pray for my baby's daddy. He's denying that this is his baby". I said, "I'll pray for you and the baby's father".

Marissa let her son come over to the apartment a couple of times. After Chase started working at the post office, the sheriff came to hand Chase child support papers for a little girl named "Tania". I asked Chase, "Why you didn't tell me about this daughter?" He told me he had another daughter, and her name is Myesha Scott. I was shocked! I said, "You have three daughters; Tysha, Myesha and Tania Scott, and one son, Dan Scott". I was mad that he didn't trust me enough to tell me. I asked, "Is there anything else shocking you might what to tell me? Tell me now. I can't believe you have all these children and didn't tell me. This makes me not trust you". Chase said, "No, I promise. There is nothing else I haven't told you".

CHAPTER 3
The Moment I Stop Breathing

Unbalanced, weak. you cannot stand. It felt like all hope is gone.

A couple of months later, Chase called me at work to tell me Marissa called him. She wanted him to buy her a gown, robe and slippers when she went to have her baby. I thought for a moment, then asked Chase, "Is this your baby?". He said it was what she was saying. I asked, "Chase, are you sleeping with her?". Chase said, "Yes, but I don't believe it's my baby. The baby could be any other guy. She sleeps with lots of them. I was shocked! I noticed my co-workers were looking through my office window staring at me. One guy knocks on my door to ask me what was wrong. I told him, "I can't talk right now. I need to go home". He asked me if I needed a ride because of the way, I looked at the time. I just needed to be alone. He asked if I needed to call my husband to come get me. I said, "I just need to go alone". He walks me to my car. He was trying to talk to me, but I couldn't talk. I got to my car, and said, "Thank you! I got to go". I drove around for hours. I made it all the way to Mississippi. I sat on the beach until morning. I called in to take the day off at work. My supervisor asked if I needed anything. I said, "No, I'll be there tomorrow". All I could think about was how I had been praying to have a baby with my husband. My husband gave my baby to another woman. I was so hurt. I couldn't talk or eat for days. I thought, "How can Marissa ask me to pray for the baby's daddy, and knew it was my husband. All I could do was pray".

Lord, help me. I can't breathe. I need you, Lord. Please help, I don't know what to do. I need your peace. Give me your peace, oh Lord. Talk to me. Tell me what to do. I need You. Lord why did you let this happen? You know I wanted a baby for many years. How could You let this happen to me? I do everything you tell me to do. How can I go on living for You knowing you let this happen to me. How long God? Please let me know what to do now. Lord, I need your strength to endure this race. Help me, Lord.

I made Chase leave. A month later, Chase came back begging for forgiveness. I told him, "I spoke with my Aunt Carol. She's an Evangelist. She told me to keep praying. I spoke with a pastor at another church because I was too embarrassed to go to our pastor. The pastor said he went through something similar. His wife slept with someone else and got pregnant for him. He prayed with me and said that God is always in control. Forgive your husband. I asked him if I should leave you. He said he couldn't tell me that, and I should ask God. Chase, I've got to pray. I can't be with you.

Just leave". Chase said, "Okay, but I'm not giving up. Leaving, he said, "I love you. I'll call you later". I said, "Please don't. I'll call you when I'm ready. Not now, maybe never. I don't know!".

God, should I take him back? God said, "Can you forgive him?". I said, Yes Lord. God said, "Take him back". I said, God, this is the hardest thing ever You've told me to do. Lord, I need your strength to endure this race. Help me, Lord.

Months passed by as I prayed about forgiving Chase. I forgave him. I called Chase, and asked him to come back home. I told him, "I forgive you, but I don't trust you". He said, I'll be working on you trusting me again". I said, "I quit my job. I'm thinking that was one of the reasons you cheated on me, because I'm making more money than you, or that I'm working with too many men. He said, "I don't sleep with her because of your job". I said, "Then why?". Chase said, "I care about her". I said, "I care about Johnny, but I won't sleep with him because I love you". Chase said, "I know, and I'm so sorry. I'm still growing". I asked, "Do you think you need more time? You've hurt me more than I can describe. If you're not ready for me, and the love I have for you, let me know now!". Chase said, "My love for you, Faith, is greater than anyone else's. I've got to be with you". I said, "Okay! I'll keep praying for you, and our marriage".

I quit my job in November. It was easy for me to find a job at a clothing store because it was so close to Christmas. I got a job at a fashion store. Chase was working nights at the Post Office. He would come into the store to bring me lunch. One day, when he walked in, there was a customer about to check out. She said, "My car is parked in the wrong place and I need to hurry". She touched my hand and said, "This time next year, you're going to be closer to where God wants you to be, then left out of the store. Chase was standing there and heard her. Chase said, "If God told her that, why didn't He tell her to pay her insurance? She wouldn't have that "no insurance" sticker on the back of her car". Chase always cracked jokes. I believed what she said. I know my faith was getting bigger. I knew God was listening to me. He knew I needed Him at that time in my life. He was letting me know I was on the right road with Him. I told Chase, "God probably told her to pay it. She didn't hear Him, kind of like you. You listen to what you want to hear".

Last year, Chase's family didn't invite me to their house for the holidays. I went to my family's house. This year was the same thing. Chase went to his family, and I went to my mine. That evening, on my way to Vera's house, I saw Johnny at the gas station. I stopped by, and we talked. He gave me his pager number. He said, "Anytime you need me, just page me. You know I will love you forever and always". I said, "Likewise".

After Christmas, the store manager asked me to be a supervisor, so I accepted. At the end of January, she asked me to be an Assistant Manager. Being an Assistant Manager meant I had to travel to other stores. When other managers would go on vacation, or had other reasons for being out, I worked it. It was fun. I'm a people person, and I love wholesale. There were good discounts for employees. My manager asked me, "What are your plans for the future?". I told her I was going to school to be an Accountant. She said, "You sure? The way you work with people, you would be a great Store Manager". I asked her what she wanted to do. She said she was going to school to be a basketball coach. I said, "You'd fit in good because you're so tall. She told me her husband and daughter were also tall. She said, "You should really think about being a Store Manager". I told her I didn't want to be a manager because Store Managers don't make enough money, but I'd think about it.

One night, Kim used Chase's car to go out with her friends. They stayed out later than usual that night. She brought it back with the gas light on. Some of her friends were boys. I asked

Kim why the boys didn't put gas in the car. I said, "Not one of those boys asked to put gas in that car?". I was so mad. I asked her why she didn't put gas in the car. She didn't give me an answer. I asked, "You can't answer me? You act like you don't care". She said, "I'm not a child". I said, "Well, why don't I have gas in this car? An adult would've put gas in a car that she borrowed". So, I told her that she had to go since she was so grown. She said, "You're putting me out?". I said, "Yes. You can't stay here with that "I don't care attitude". I have enough going on with Chase and his drama. I don't want to put up with you not respecting me. I've given you a place to stay, and a car to drive. Now, you want to disrespect me? I can't take this from you. go!"

Kim called her friend to stay with her, and she left. Months after I put Kim out, she graduated from high school, and already pregnant. She was looking for a job. I helped her get a job at the fashion store.

When Chase moved back in, we were talking about how we could do better as a couple. I said, I'm not good enough for you". Chase said, "I couldn't ask for no one better. You're the wife all men look for". I said, "Why you make me out to be less than the best?" He said, "It's not you, it's me. I need more growing up". We talked for hours, then decided to move away from here. I said, "Where will we go?". Chase said, "I got a friend in Atlanta, GA. Let's move there. I think we can grow in that big town. We can get more accomplished. More money is there, and more opportunities. Let's go". Little did I know that his opportunities were not the ones I wanted. I said, "We need to move in with someone here to save money". I called Vera, and asked if could we stay with her until we moved to Georgia. She said, "Yes, you sure can stay here if you're sure about moving to a big city with Chase, of all people". I said, "I know he's not trust worthy, but I'm going to try to make this marriage work. I know that's what God wants me to do".

I was always watching a Christian network channel. It was nationwide, and aired pastors from all over the country. There was this one pastor in College Park, GA. He would get me all stirred up, and ready to move on to the next day. When I'd watch him, I'd say, "I got to get to that church".

This was in the late 90's. At that time, he was in a small church in College Park. I never thought I'd move, and live in Georgia to visit that church.

Chase called one of his friends, Goody, that lived in Georgia. He asked him if we could stay with him until we could get an apartment. He said we could. We stayed with Vera for six months. I finally finished school, and received an Associate Degree in Accounting. Chase and I quit our jobs, and prepared to move. We only packed suitcases of clothes until we could find an apartment, then we'd come back to get our furniture, etc.

The weekend before we moved, my girlfriend, Taura, was getting married. She lived in Georgia, so she came home to get married. Her fiancé was from Georgia. I thought that was awesome. Georgia was new to me, but she'd been living there for a while. She'd be able to tell me where to find a job. I told her Chase's friend lived in Lithia Springs, GA, and that's where we would be staying. Taura said that town was not far from her.

They stayed in Douglasville, GA which was one exit from us. I said, "That's good. I'm going to need your help".

The same month of Taura's wedding, my father died. He had liver cancer. My father was an alcoholic. When he got saved, he stopped drinking. Chase and I got to the church for the funeral. As we were getting out of the car, the family was about to walk in the church. They were watching Chase and I walk up as if we were stars. When we got to the door, they asked, "Who are you walking up here like that?" I said, "Like what?" "Y'all looking like movie stars" one said. I said, "We have on black just like y'all". One of my cousins said, "It's the way you look in black as you walk up here to the church". I didn't know what to say. I looked surprised, and said, "Sorry, I didn't mean any harm". He said, "Come on girl, let's go inside". We went in, and I viewed his body, but I didn't know how to take his death. I loved him so much. I just didn't know what to think or say about his death.

I was very excited about this new change. I've never left the state of Louisiana to live elsewhere. Once we got to Georgia, I met Chase's friend, Goody, and his wife. I saw instantly she didn't like me. I said, Hi. Nice to meet you". Maybe I should have said, I'm sorry that I'm smaller than you, and I don't want your husband". I don't know. All I know was I couldn't stay there long. We all sat and talked for a while before going to bed. We arrived on a Sunday. Monday, Goody helped Chase get a job at the plant. Chase said he wasn't going to stay long because it wasn't enough money. Chase started working part time at an office supply store. Chase said he wished he could've transferred from the post office in Baton Rouge to the post office there. I said, "You can still go apply. You just need a little faith.

God can make it happen". Chase said, "You have faith, so I'll go apply".

It's December, and I'm looking for a place to stay and a job. Goody's wife said they were hiring cashiers where she worked. I said, "Tell me where to apply for the job". She helped me get a job at the arts and craft store. While waiting to start my new job, I went to a bank, and applied for a teller's position. I got an interview and was hired the same day. The bank job didn't start until January 15th.

Now, I am working at an arts and craft store while waiting to start at the bank. I also was able find an apartment.

We went back to Louisiana to get our furniture and things. Once we came back to Georgia, I started training at the bank shortly after. Once training started, I quit my other job. I was going to keep both jobs, but the distance was too far apart. Chase was working at the plant with Goody during the day, and the office supply store at night. Everything seemed to be going well until I received a call from my cousin. She told me Chase had been calling her. She said, "When he gets back home, he wants to sleep with me". I said, "Why does he want to sleep with you?". I know she can say things in a way that he may have misunderstood or she misunderstood him. He may have thought she was coming on to him. I asked her, "How long have you been talking to him?". She said, "Before y'all moved to Georgia. I had to tell you". I said, "Why are you telling me now? Do you want him?". She said, "No, I don't". I said, "Thank you for telling me. I'll talk to you later". When Chase came home, I asked him why he wanted to cheat on me with my cousin. He said, "She's lying". I said, "No, she's not. Why you can't stop doing me wrong? I love you, but you want any woman who will agree to sleep with you. We just got here to start over. It seems like you came here to see what you can do wrong here. I don't know how to make you happy. We make love at least four times a week. We go at least an hour at a time. How much is enough for you?". Chase said, "I want it all day, every day". I said, "Why didn't you tell me this in the beginning? I wouldn't have agreed to marry you. You're making this so hard for me. I don't feel I want this anymore. I'll continue praying for you. I hope God gives me an ending to this relationship". Little did I know, it was just getting started.

Chase left out of the apartment after our argument. I paged Johnny, and he called me. I told him my husband was cheating again with my cousin.

Johnny said, "Faith, just hold on. God has a plan. I know you are strong. God wouldn't have put you there to leave you. Just hold on. Everything is going to be alright". I said, "I know I need to hold on, but why should I when he doesn't seem to care about me? He makes it all about him. I don't think I'm that strong to hold on. Johnny, thank you for encouraging me".

New Church Home

God wants us to assemble so that we can help one another. As a Christian, this is very important. Do not forsake the assembly. Heb 10:25

I called Taura to ask her about her church. I needed to go to a teaching church. Taura and I grew up together. We lived on the same street, and we went to the same elementary school. We are the same age, and attended the same Baptist church. Taura told me about her church. She asked if I wanted to go with her. I said, "Yes", then asked her about the pastor at College Park. She said, " A lot of the people that go there are big timers. They have big houses and cars. They are cocky and arrogant. You don't want to go there". I said, "Okay". I went to church with her. Her husband wasn't going, and neither was Chase. I said to Taura, "I've been going here a month. I want to become a member, but I know I have to go to College Park Church first".

Taura said, "Lots of people don't want to go to his church. They said he takes the people's money.

Everyone that goes there has BMW's, Mercedes, or real expensive cars. The pastor drives a Bentley".

In my mind I thinking, "If they have that much money, I must check this out. I don't know why, but I think I need to go there".

I started working at the Bank as a teller. I was promoted to helping people with their accounts, and do start up accounts for new customers. I was trying to work on becoming a Branch Manager.

Months passed by. I asked my co-worker where was College Park. She directed me, then asked why. I said, "I want to go to College Park Church". She said, "Girl, they're going to take your money. Do you know he drives a Bentley?". I said, "I heard that, but I still want to go". She gave me directions. Sunday came. I was on my way to Taura's church, but for some reason, I couldn't get over to the exit ramp. I told myself, "I'll get off at the next exit". I got to the next exit, but no one would let me over. In Georgia, the exits are like ten miles apart. I was getting to the next exit, but I had to go around a curve, then get off. There was so much traffic. I just followed it. The traffic led me right to the church I wanted to find. I was surprised! I was looking for the small church I saw on TV. It was a big dome that was just built. The small church was about a ¼ mile from the front door of the dome. I was surprised how I had finally made it to College Park Church, and the way I made it was amazing. It wasn't in my plan. God had it all under control. It took about 15 minutes to park, and walk to the door. The ushers were handing out tissues. I never saw that ever done in a church. I walked in, and saw so many people with their faces on the floor.

They were just lying there, stretched out on the floor. I took about two more steps, and fell to the floor. I heard God say, "This is your home". I finally got up, and walked into the sanctuary. I felt God's presence strongly for the very first time in a while. I didn't want to leave. I sat down, heard the message, and joined the church. I had to take sixteen weeks of classes before I could become a member. That was the best sixteen weeks of my life! I learned so much about God. Finally, I was getting used by God. I didn't think or know God was so powerful. He wanted to use me. I couldn't believe He wanted me!

I remember going to get my hair cut. The night before, I read the book of Ecclesiastes. I don't know why I read that book. As I was walking to the barber shop, I passed by a beauty salon. I never paid any attention to it before. God told me to go in there. I did, and there was only one beautician, and no customers. He said, "Can I help you?". I said, "I don't know". I told him I was going next door to get my hair cut. He said, "I can cut your hair". I sat in the chair, and he began cutting my hair. I was talking to him about what I read the night before, in the book of Ecclesiastes, having a time and chance for everything. I said more, but can't remember what. Before I knew it, he was on the floor. I tried to wake him up. Finally, he wakes up and says, "I needed that". I said, "What, a nap?". He said, "No, what you said to me". I said, "Oh! That was all God". He said, "It had to be". He looked at my hair, and saw he had jacked it up. He had holes everywhere. He said, "I'll fix it for you. Come back next week, and I'll work on it. I had to wear a hat or scarf to cover it up. God said, "I didn't tell you to get your hair cut". The barber gave me some shampoo to wash my hair, and to come back next Friday. I said, "Okay".

I went back to the salon the next Friday. He took off my scarf. He was looking at the back of my head. In the mirror, I could see his surprised face. I said, "What's wrong?". He said, "What did you do?". He gave me a hand-held mirror to look at my head. I said, "It looks better than it did before you cut it". It looked as if he had never touched my head. I said, "God is so amazing". I thanked the barber, blessed him, and left. God used me on another occasion. As I was shopping, a lady passing by me. I heard God say, "Tell her I love her". I told the lady, "God says He loves you". She looked shocked and began crying. She said, "I needed to hear that".

Another time, it became evident God was using me. After spending time in the Bible, I went to bring Chase some lunch at work. I walked in the door, and people were looking at me as if I was someone very important or a movie star. They moved out of my way, and stepped aside when I passed them. Chase seemed nervous, so I thought he was going to tell me something was wrong with me. He introduced me to his managers and co-workers. They were all looking at me with amazement. I felt so uncomfortable. I handed Chase his lunch, said bye, then walked out of the store. As I walked out the door, God said, "My glory is all over you." I was in awe the rest of the day. I couldn't believe God loved me that way.

When I returned home, all I could do was sing and dance. I danced, and didn't know I could dance like that. I moved stuff out of the way, and danced until I got sleepy.

I asked Chase if he wanted to go to church with me that night. He said, "Yes". It was a Friday night service. Chase didn't know that so many people went to church for a Friday service. Chase was in awe of the dome. He said, "I think I'm going to like it here". That night, the pastor was prophesying.

He said, "There are some men I need to speak to tonight". He called certain men up. Then he said, "There's one more, and you know who you are. It's you", and he pointed our way. "You, the man with the long sleeve white shirt". He was pointing at Chase. Chase went up, and the pastor said, "God sent you here. You're an anointed man of God.

You're a great minister. God has work for you to do". He came back to his seat, and said, "My grandmother said the same thing". I said, "Well, let's get started doing the work for God together". Chase came to church with me every Sunday for about three months, then he stopped.

When we first got together, Chase taught me there are sixty-six books in the Bible. He grew up Catholic, but went to a Christian school all his school years. I'd even see God using him on his jobs. I don't understand how he wouldn't want to give God all of him. Although he was Catholic, and attending a different school with different beliefs, I thought he would've received something that would make him want God more than me.

Chase said, "Suppose we do all this studying, and believe all that is in the Bible. We die, and there is no God". I said, "I just believe in God. I never imagined doing what God has me to do and feeling how I feel. When I read the Bible, there is a great God. In fact, I want to die today, right now to be with Him. There's no feeling like the feeling God has given me. No man has ever made me feel this way, and I have dated a lot of men".

Chase wanted to try to get a job at the post office there. I said, "You'll get the job". Chase said, "Faith, it's not the same as the post office in Baton Rouge. I said, "You are going to get that job".

Chase said, "I might get the job. It's hard not being in a position as a Regular in the post office". I said, "It won't be hard for you". "Faith, you know it takes years for people to become a Regular at the Post Office, he added. I said, "You need to stop listening to other people. I know you don't trust God as I do. In the natural, you're one who will most likely make it anywhere, doing anything. You should believe that. Just go and apply and see for yourself". He said, "Faith, you don't know how it took my mama years. I know it's going to take me longer". I finally said, "I have the faith that God is going to get you that job. Just go apply".

Chase applied for the post office, and got an interview. He got a letter stating that he got the job. Not only did he get the job, he got a Regular position. He told me it was impossible to get that position. He couldn't believe it. I said, "Chase the faith I have, I believed God would make it happen. You can too. He put you in a position you said would never happen". Chase said, "I can't wait to get home to tell them I am a Regular. Faith, you must have prayed". I said, "I pray for you every day". Chase quit the plant and the office supply store, and started working at the post office. I said, "Chase, God is building your faith. This is just the beginning".

My job was so boring. I didn't want to work there anymore until they made it exciting to stay. They said we were going into three groups. The group that gets the most people to get a bank card in a month wins a lunch at a fine restaurant. I thought, "It is on now!". My group won, but I still did not feel like I wanted to be there. I'm an accountant, and I always liked working with numbers. I took a break and went read my Bible. Looking through there was a lot of numbers. The fourth book of the Bible is called Numbers. Four represents a new being, eight, a new beginning. So, every four days, weeks, and months has a new beginning. I thought it was awesome to know. The number "Forty" is also big and broad all over Bible. Also, "One hundred, forty-four is big. All these numbers are just something I needed to study. I thought, "Maybe I need a ministry job". My grandmother prophesied to me that I am a Women of God. I just may need to go back to school, or maybe not. I hate school, although, ministry school could be different.

Weeks later, Chase and I were leaving out the same time. I said, "I've got to get gas". Chase said, "I'll get gas. You take my car. I will take your car today". When I got home that night, the phone rang, so I answered the call. A girl said, "Tell Chase I wrecked his car". I said, "That is not Chase's car, that is my car". She said, "Anyway, it's wrecked. Tell him to come get it". I couldn't believe Chase would let one of his girls drive my car. When Chase came home, I said, "I'm tired of you. It is girl after girl. Why don't you let me go? Please! I beg you to let me go, so I can move on to someone who will truly love me". We began arguing. He went to the bathroom. I pushed him in the tub. When he fell back, he fell on his arm. He thought it was broken. I took him to the hospital. It wasn't broken, it was sprained. That didn't stop him. He would leave on a Thursday, and not come back for days. I was so tired of Chase treating me like I was not his wife. I was ready to go back home. After talking myself in to leaving, I began packing my things. I thought, "I want to be working. I am just going to serve God until He gives me the okay to go back home". I never read the whole Bible before.

That morning, I started to reading. I told myself I was going to read the Bible from Genesis to Revelation. Maybe, I would see something that would help me through this trial. I started reading Genesis. When I got to Chapter 13 reading about Abram, it felt like I got out of my body and began walking with Abram. I could clearly see everything around him. It was amazing. That day, I read to the Book of Numbers. I never liked to read, but

I was so interested in the Bible. I read until dark. I took a bath and started praying in tongues. I felt so good. I didn't realize Chase wasn't there. The next morning, I got up, made me a cup of coffee, and ate some grits and eggs. I started to reading again. It felt like I was there. I read until dark. I got up, turned on the music, and began dancing like a jazz dancer. I didn't know I could do that. Spending time with God, I began seeing who I am and what I am.

Chase didn't come home until Thursday night. He walked in and asked me if I wanted to go get something to eat, as if he had been there all week. I told him I put in my two-week notice. He said, "Okay. Do you want to get something to eat?". I said, "No, I want to go back home because I can be alone there. He acted as if I didn't tell him I was packed and ready to go back home. Chase said, "You will change your mind". I said, "No, not this time. I'm just waiting on God's okay". He said, " Alright, you just wait on God. I'm going get something to eat". When he got back, he said," I brought you something". I said, Thanks, but I'm not hungry". He said, "We have no food here.

What did you eat?". I said, "God! God fed me enough". Chase said, "Whatever Faith, whatever".

It was weeks before I got a call from anyone, or even talk to anyone other than God. I was so deep into what I was reading. I never read a book this way. I began acting out whatever I was reading. I was preforming with Moses hitting the rock. It was like I went with Moses to hit the rock. Then later, when God told Moses to speak to the rock, Moses was going to hit the rock. I was jumping up and down to let him know God said to speak to that rock, not hit it. He didn't see me. Moses hit the rock. This showed me that we are disobedient at least one time in our lives. In the book of Leviticus, people were complaining so much about the same things over and over. I was like, "Shut up, and stop complaining". I thought, "Why am I complaining? God is supplying all my needs. I quit my job, and I wasn't paying any bills. God fixed money for Chase. Chase is diligently paying all the bills, and making sure I have everything I need". I said, "God, I repent, Lord. I am truly sorry for complaining. I want You to deliver me from this angry state of mind. I don't want to live with this anger. In Jesus Name, Amen".

Later, that week, I met with Taura and her husband. We had gone to the park to see a jazz concert. Taura asked where was Chase. I said, "I don't know". Taura husband asked me, "How could God let someone saved go through all you've been through?". I said, "I don't know. I do know He has everything under control". That weekend was one of my best weekends I had in a long time. I had a great time with Taura and her husband. We explored Atlanta seeing things I've never seen before. It felt so good. I almost didn't want to go home, but I knew one of these days, Chase will be there to, hopefully, make me happy. I just knew he'd be back. When I got home, no Chase. I thought, "I'm still packed and ready to go, Lord".

Weeks later after that drama, Johnny paged me. I called him. He told me he was getting married. I asked him, "Are you sure this is your wife?". He said, "I think so. I just needed to page you to let you know. Faith, you are my best friend". I said, "What do you need me to be, your best man?". He laughed and said, "No. I'm just letting you know". I said, "Okay, thank you for letting me know.

When are you getting married?". He said, "Sunday". I said, "Sunday is not a wedding day". He said, "I know, but that's when the pastor can marry us". I said, "Today is Thursday. Why you just paging me now?" He said, "She wanted it this Sunday". Chase had not come home yet. I really didn't know where he was. I left him a note saying I was going home to Baton Rouge for the weekend. While driving back home, I was thinking why he wanted to get married now. Why not wait a little while? I wanted to leave Chase, and Johnny wanted to get married. Johnny is my best friend.

Once I returned to Baton Rouge, I paged Johnny, and he met me at Vera's house around 4:00pm. He showed me the ring, it was a two-carat diamond.

He said, "The reason why she wants to get married now is because she's taking her children to an amusement park in Florida, and I'm not going. I guess she wants to make sure I'll be here when she gets back". I said, "How long will she be staying?" He said, "A week". Well, did you tell her you'll be here when she gets back?", I asked. He said, "I reassured her, but she still wants to get married tomorrow". I asked how many children she had.

He said, "Five". I said, "You and I always wanted a family. I guess you'll get yours that way. I got mine Chase's way". I didn't tell him what Chase and I was going through, or that I wanted a life with him. I just told him, "I'll always love you. Go and be happy with your new wife".

First Time God Audibly Speaks

At Gibeon, the Lord appeared to Solomon during the night in a dream, and God said, "Ask for whatever you want me to give you." I Kings 3:5

November, 1998, Taura came over to ask me if I wanted to go to a Bible study at her friend Rose's house. I said, "No, I'm going back home. I can't take this cheating anymore. I'm just waiting on God to answer me". She said, "While you wait, we should go to Rose's Bible Study. You might hear from God there". I agreed. I needed that. Rose opened the door. She looked at me and said, "Unpack your bags. It's not time yet." I thought, "You don't know me". I sat down. We had Bible study. I don't know what she said after she told me to unpack. Bible Study was over, and we were about to leave. Rose said, "We need to have Bible Study at your house next week". I said, "Okay, I'll get things ready". After we left, I told Taura, "I didn't want to go, and now I must have Bible Study at my place". She said, "Isn't God good?". I said, "Shut-up! A week passed, and weeks turned into months.

One Sunday after I left church, I went home. I saw Chase on the sofa. I walked to the back to take a nap. After dozing off, I heard God say, "Wake up". I woke up. Once I was awake, He said, "You're going to speak at Bible study Wednesday". I said, "I don't know what to say". He said, "I'll tell you". I went to my computer and began typing. I typed three paragraphs. I read it, printed it, and asked Chase to read it. He said take this and that out. I took those things out, then I printed it again.

Wednesday came. I was so nervous. I spoke, and thought it was okay. Rose said, "You should expound on that next week". The following week, I started with what I spoke on the previous week, then I talked about what Chase told me to take out. One of the ladies said, "Why you didn't say that last week? I needed that last week the most". I told her I was sorry. At that time, I learned whatever God tells me to do, and however it might sound like, just do it. I told the ladies in the meeting what had happened with the notes last week to let them know I was learning to do what God said, no matter what! One lady said, "You should talk about that next week about how we must do what God says, no matter what". I agreed, and I did that teaching the next week.

Those weeks turned into six months. Rose came in the next week prophesying to me. She said, "You're anointed to heal. God is going to use you mightily. He said be bold, and dance for Him". I was shocked. I never danced in front of people. I started doing the "Bank Head Bounce" dance. I know that's not what He was talking about. When everyone left, I began doing a jazz dance. When He asked me to dance for Him, I didn't want to because people would watch. That dance was for me and God only. I danced for hours until I fell asleep.

God told me I was a minister of healing. I started studying about healing. I learned healing was very broad. What kind of healing was I to do? Maybe its physical healing, or maybe it's my marriage. The Lord knows I can testify about that. I heard God say, "You are a minister of it all". That blew my mind. I didn't know He was listening. God was always blowing my mind.

Days later, I went to a clothing store. When I walked in, a sales clerk asked, if could she help me. As we walked together, I said, 'I am looking for some shoes". I saw a pair I liked, then said, "I need this in an 8 1/2". She said, "You are so beautiful". I said, "Thank you. She went grab the shoes. We began talking, and God came up. She was going through something at the time. So, I prayed for the stuff she was going through. She asked me what kind of work I did. I said, "The last job was in a bank. She said, "So, you're not working now?". I told her I wasn't, she said, "Come work here". I said, "If you need someone in shoes, I would never have any money. She laughed and said, "No, I need a customer service person.

I'm a Human Resource Manager, and I'll hire you". I said, "Okay", I started working the next day. I was making $10 an hour as a customer service representative, and we were paid every week. I loved it. The bill collectors began calling. In about a year, no bill collectors called. The whole time I had no job, nobody called. As soon as I got a job, they start calling. The light company, phone company and the car company called. I was paying my car note and saving money to go back home. I worked there about four months.

I figured out the reason I moved to Georgia. It wasn't about my marriage to Chase, but my marriage to Jesus! I loved that I learned so much about myself, my purpose, and where I was supposed to be right then in my life. It was all a "God" set up! Everything I experienced here with God; Madea told me it would happen. Right down to the time she saw me on an airplane wearing a red blouse. My first time on a plane was when I flew to Baton Rouge. I would fly back home to get food to cook. When I was returning to Atlanta, I had on a red blouse. I remembered what Madea said when I was a child. I thank God for my Madea revealing my future to me as a little girl. She taught me the beginning of this journey. Now, it was up to me to continue until this journey is completed. I don't know how long I'd have to put up with no family, and all this unhappiness with this husband of mine. I did know I'd hold on until God set me free.

I was still packed and ready to go back home. Chase was still leaving one day, and coming home days later.

I Finally Get My Answer

I learned on this day, whatever you ask God for, He will answer. A lot of people think when you pray for something, you should keep praying for it. God heard you the first time. Just remember, with faith you have what you asked. Just start thanking Him and worshipping Him for it. It will come in His time, not yours. *If you believe, you will receive whatever you ask for in prayer. Matt. 21:22*

Monday, I prayed and asked God if it would be okay for me to go back home. I didn't get an answer that day. I continued praising and worshipping God. On Wednesday, Chase asked me out to dinner. I said, "Okay". At the restaurant, we talked about how unhappy I was with our relationship. Chase said he would do better. The next night, Chase left and didn't come back again. I went to church for the Friday night service. I was so happy praising and worshipping God. I heard God's voice so clearly as if there was no music. He said, *"I will be with you when you go back to Baton Rouge"*. I was so excited to hear His voice. I asked the lady next to me if she heard Him. She said, "No, the music is too loud". I knew the music was loud, but I heard God louder and clearer than ever. The next morning when I woke up, I noticed Chase didn't come home the night before. I put all my packed things in the car. I got breakfast, gassed up, and headed back home to Baton Rouge. I couldn't tell Chase in person that I thought our marriage was over, so I left him a note. I told him I was going home. It was the 4th of July.

Marriage is a journey you never know where you're going or what is going to happen. Month by month, year by year, you must wait and see. You should always pay attention to your surroundings. That includes people, places and all situations.

CHAPTER 4
GOING THROUGH THE HURT

Back in Baton Rouge. I moved in with Evan and his new wife. Chase called looking for me. He said, "I thought you were just moving your clothes to Taura's house and staying with her". I said, "Chase, my clothes were packed for months. I told you I don't want to live this way anymore". He said, "I can't just let leave this marriage. I won't let you leave". I said, "I'm gone and there's nothing you can do now". He said, "What about God? Did you ask Him?". I answered, "Yes, I did, and He said He will be with me. I'm coming back to get my furniture when I find a storage unit".

Two weeks later, Chase was at my brother's house begging me to not end our marriage. He said, "I miss you, and I need you". I said, "Chase, you didn't need me when I was there because you were never there". "Faith, I'm sorry I wronged you. I need us to be together", he said. I said, "Why Chase? So, you can have security? I don't understand you. You don't need me financially.

You sleep with everybody in and out of Atlanta. It can't be compassion. I don't think you even know what that means. Is it that you can just say you are married? Is that how you get your women, by saying you have a bad marriage?". He said, "No, I love you! That's why I want this marriage". I said, "Chase, do you even know what love is? If this is love, you don't need me. My kind of love is a strong, compassionate, and kind man. That's what I saw in you when I married you. When you showed me your kindness and compassion, that's what I fell in love with, not the physical stuff. I don't know you anymore. You manipulate people into thinking you're someone you're not. I thought we were starting a new life in Atlanta. You made it worse by making a baby with another woman when you knew I wanted a baby. You hurt me continually. I don't need you nor want you anymore". Chase went back to Georgia the next day.

I started looking for a job. I got a part-time job at a clothing store making $6.50 an hour for the same company I worked for in Atlanta, but less money. It was okay. I needed a job. I worked nights, so I looked for a full-time job to work days, like accounting or something dealing with money. I couldn't go back to a bank. It was boring doing the same thing day in and day out. My cousin called to ask if I would like to work with her doing medical billing at The General Hospital. I told her I thought it was exactly what I needed. I interviewed, and got the job making $10.00 an hour. I worked a little longer at the clothing store to save money.

After I got well rounded in billing, I quit the clothing store.

I started attending the church we went to when we were first married. I shared what I learned in Georgia about myself. The more I spoke about God, the more I could see Him using me. I prayed in tongues more often. Praying in tongues takes me to a place I want to be with God. This new job was an opportunity to share what I knew about the Bible. I learned everything I could about billing insurances. Making more money has always been my goal. Moving to the accounting department was going to do that. Medicare is the base to all insurance companies. I learned the rules to Medicare, so I could get promoted to Accounting, which I did. I attended an annual class which taught me insurance updates. I wanted to be on top. I was never close to my cousin who helped me get the job, but we became friends at work. I learned we had many things in common. I believe getting stronger in Him, and being all, I can be is something God put in me. My cousin was a part of my accomplishments at work, and I will always love her for that.

Chase was trying to reach me to let me know he was transferring to a post office in Baton Rouge. I didn't care. I was looking for an apartment or house to rent, so Chase couldn't find me.

Everything was going well for me. After I found a house, I called Chase to tell him I was coming to get my furniture. He was so excited. I told him I'd be bringing Fredrick to help me. I rented a truck, and headed to Georgia with Fredrick. Everybody all over the world was preparing for Y2K. Computers were supposed mal-function. I remember President Bush ordering money to be printed because there was a possibility banks would have problems with money. The President couldn't have that. He was a Republican, and you don't mess with their money. We got my stuff and came home with no problems.

I wanted to go to ministry school. The school I was wanting to attend was affiliated with my pastor in College Park, GA. I asked my pastor at the church I was attending at the time if he thought it, was a good school. He said it was, so I enrolled. Chase got the transfer to Baton Rouge Post Office, and went stay with his mama. Chase called me to let me know he was back in Baton Rouge working at the post office as a Regular. He said, "you told me that was going to happen. You said, where I go, I will prosper. Thank you for telling me that". I said, "No, you should thank God because nothing He does is an accident. Chase, I can't help that I have faith". I told him I had to go to a meeting at the ministry school. I asked him if wanted to go.

He said he would like to go. After the meeting, one of my teachers came over to meet Chase. He shook Chase's hand and said, "You are anointed. You're supposed to be here with your wife". Chase said, "Maybe, maybe not. I'm not ready". The teacher said, "Time waits for no one". Chase met the rest of my teachers, then we left. On the way home, Chase said, "Why God wants me?". I said, "I don't know. I know I surely don't want you", then we laughed. Chase saw a restaurant, so we stopped to eat. We talked for a while. He said, "I want my wife back". I said, "God didn't tell me that I must take you back. If you would walk the way He wants you to walk, He would talk to you and show you things". Chase asked me, "Did you ask God to take me back?". I said, "No, I don't want the Chase back that you have become. I want the Chase that is compassionate, and the man that showed me he loved me. That is the Chase I need now.

At this point, I'm in my new place to live. I put on some praise and worship songs. I started praying in tongues and speaking out scriptures. "The race is not given to the swift or strong, it's given to the ones who endure to the end". I began praying for Chase and the call God had on him. I prayed for his faith in God to grow. I asked God to teach me more about Him, so if Chase and I got back together. I would be stronger.

I paged Johnny, and gave him my number. He called and came over that morning. I was sewing some curtains. We talked about his marriage. He said she was a gambler, and he was tired of looking for her. When he'd find her, she'd be at the casino boats. I asked, "Where are the children?".

He said, "At home. They keep each other company when I'm not there". "How old is the oldest?", I asked. He said, " Fifteen. I can't sleep there with all that fussing and fighting. I need somewhere to sleep". I told him to go sleep in the room I fixed for my nieces and nephews. I finished sewing my curtains, then I went grocery shopping. I cooked pork chops and gravy with green beans. Johnny slept about six hours. When he got up, I asked him if wanted what I cooked. He said, "I think that's why I woke up. I smell food". After he ate, I told him I'd be praying for his wife and her kids, but for him to take care of the kids while she was going through her problem.

That night, Chase called asking if I'd like to go to lunch with him when I got out of church the next day. I agreed. I got to church, and he was there before me. I couldn't believe it. We went to lunch and talked. He wanted to know where I lived. I wouldn't tell him. I was still waiting on God. We were together all day. We went to the mall. He wanted to buy me something. I told him time and time again, that's not the man I need. I said, "I need you to go back in your mind to the beginning of our relationship to find out what I wanted at that time from a man, then you will know me. If I want things. I can buy them myself". We had a good day just like I always wanted. It was almost like the beginning of our relationship was. He enjoyed it too. He wanted to take a ride to New Orleans. We got to New Orleans, went ate beignets and drank coffee. It was fun, but not enough to bring him to my house. We got a room at the Marriot

Hotel in New Orleans. We both called in sick to work the next day, and shopped in New Orleans while we talked more about our marriage and God. The God part was very revealing to me. He said he wanted God in his life more. We prayed. I know Chase so well. He wanted so bad to find out where I lived.

He thought he could bring God in the conversation, and it would help to get him there. Chase was always manipulative, so I knew what he was up to. We ate dinner, then headed back home. I took him to his car, and went home. I had a great time with Chase. I wished it wouldn't have ended.

I was the co-worker who would get birthday cakes and presents for everyone on their birthday. I'd try to make each one's birthday special. Everyone would talk about their birthday as if it was the event of the year. I never felt that way about my birthday. I wanted everyone else to have a special day of the year. I found out what each liked or needed, and their favorite colors. I had to decorate their work area. Co-workers would pass by and recognize their special day. Then, my birthday rolled around. I expressed before we began the birthday collection that I don't care about my birthday. Just get a cake so we can share it. They didn't listen. I had decorations including balloons, lunch, cake, and presents given to me with a big angel figurine. They said, "Because you have made all our birthdays special, we all wanted to give you something very special. You just don't bring us gifts. You bring God too. So, we got this angel for you. We love you Faith". I wanted to cry. I felt so special. I said, "I didn't know I made y'all feel like this. Thank you so much. Now, I understand why people love their birthdays". That was my 31st birthday, and it was the best one ever.

Back Together Again

Four months later, I finally told Chase where I lived. He had a hard time finding it. He had never been in that part of town. He got so frustrated looking that night. I said, "Don't worry about coming tonight. I'll come get you tomorrow and you can follow me". He said, "No, I'll find it tonight". After, an hour, he showed up. He said, "This is a good hiding place. I would have never come back here. I don't understand, with all the good and expensive things you like, why would you live here?". I said, "I could live in a shot gun house here in the hood, and make it look like a mansion. If I'm happy, it doesn't matter where I live. Chase, can you make me happy?". He said, "Yes Faith, I can make you happy". I said, "Sleeping with all those other women is not the way to make me happy." Chase replied, "I know. Let's start a new beginning". I said, "How will you start a new beginning? Please tell me how because

I thought going to Atlanta was starting a new beginning? You continue to cheat on another level. Did you know Atlanta has the most cases of HIV virus? Before I make love to you, you must take a HIV test, and I'm going with you because I don't trust you. I don't know how long it will be when I do trust you again". Chase told me to make an appointment. We both got tested. Six weeks later, we got the results. It was negative for the both of us. As we were on the way home, Chase stopped at a hotel. I said, "What are you doing?". He said, "It's going to take too long to get home. I need you right now!". We both laughed. We got a room, ordered food, and stayed all night.

I told Chase one of my teacher's prophesied to me. He said that God told him I was going to get a house. Chase said, "That's a good new start for us". I said, "God said I'm going to get a house, not you!". Chase laughed, but I wasn't laughing. The next weekend, I began looking for a house. I wanted a nice neighborhood with white and black people in the new subdivision. All the new houses had small bedrooms and open floor plans. I wanted big bedrooms. I started looking in old subdivisions.

The rooms were much bigger, but the price was very high. One of my friends told me to get a real estate agent. I started calling some of the small real estate companies, not wanting to go with a big one. I found a black owned company called "Ceegee Realty". I made an appointment with them. When I met with the agent, she did a credit check on me. She told me there were a couple things I needed to work on to get my score up. She said, "Right now, you are qualified for $80,000. Your house note will be an average of $650-$750. That's not including escrow which includes insurance and property taxes". I knew that note was very high for me, but God said He was going to get me a house. I knew He would not let me down. I started fixing my credit issues. While doing that, my agent and I started looking for an older house with big rooms and two bathrooms. I found one I liked. She said I should put in an offer. She filled out the paper work and put in the offer. We found out later that day that someone else had put in an offer. She said I needed to counter offer. She explained that it meant we either go up on the price, or pay closing cost. She suggested an offer, I said okay, and she made the offer. At that time, the person sold the house already. We started looking again. We found another house, and put in an offer. It was sold. She said she would check the internet for listings. I continued working on my credit. I got two of the problems solved. While I'm working on the last one, I began praying, "Lord, I know You have never given me a task I could not accomplish. Lord, I am discouraged because I do not know what to do. The house I like was sold. I need your help. I cannot do this alone.

Lord, help me to get the house you want me to have. You said I can have what I ask if I just believe it. I believe and receive it".

I started singing my favorite song, "The race is not given to the swift or the strong, but to the ones who endure." The next day, my agent called saying she had a house for me. She asked, "When can you meet me to see it?". I said, "Later today. Where is it located?". She said, "It is in an old subdivision, but the price is higher than what you are qualified for. It's going for $120,000". I said, "How much would the note be?". "$1,184 a month", she said. I said, "Oh my God!". She said, "I believe God has a lot to do with it". I met her at the house. It was on a corner lot with a big yard. I remembered when I was younger, Madea said I would have a house on the corner. We walked through the front door, and I heard God voice, "This is your house". I stopped in the foyer, and the agent asked what was wrong. I said, "This is my house". She said, "You haven't seen all of it". I said, "I don't have to. Where are the papers to make an offer?". I was in awe! She said, "Come on, you got to see the rest of the house". I said, "I will. How much money do I need to put down?". She said, "$300-$500. You can write a check, and we'll hold it until you get the house". I gave her a $300.00 check, then looked at the rest of the house. After I saw every inch of it, I went outside in the backyard, and said, "God, all this is for me?". He said, "Yes". I said to the agent, "Let's go so I can put in an offer". When we got to the office, the agent told the owner I wanted to make an offer on the West Darryl house. The owner said, "We have been trying to sell that house for almost two years". I said, "What's wrong with it?". She said, "Nothing". I couldn't believe it. The house was so beautiful to me. The owner looked at all my paperwork and said, "You're going to have to put down $8,500.00. I didn't have that much money in the bank. I only had my bill, gas and food money. It was exactly $563.00. I told her I didn't have that much money. She said I had 30 days to get it. I headed to my car. When I got in, I asked God what was I going to do. I went to Vera's house, so excited, I told Vera, Carla and Kim about the house. They wanted to see it. I took them to see it. They were excited. I brought them back and called Chase. I told him I had found my house. He asked when could he come to see it. I said, "Tomorrow. I will get the agent to open the door". The next day, Chase and I went to the house. I told him God said this was my house. I introduced Chase to the agent. She said, "You didn't say you were married". I said, "Because God said He was going to give me a house". The agent said, "God never does anything out of order. I'm sure He was talking about you and your husband". I told her we were not back together, yet. She said, "Maybe God is giving you this house to help y'all to get back together". I said, "Maybe". Chase was ready to see the house. He got inside and was in awe.

Chase said, "Faith, "You want this house?". I said, "Yes". He said, "Okay. What do I need to do to help you get this house?". The agent said, "We have to do a credit check on you. Because you are married, the house is going to be for the both of you". Chase and I went to the office, did the paper work, and ran his credit score. His score was higher than mine. He qualified for $150,000 which was very good. When we left, Chase said, "We don't have that kind of money for the down payment". I told him we had thirty days. We got back together, and got our hustle on. I saved my checks and half of Chase's checks. I filed my taxes for that year and got back $2,500. It was a miracle because I never got that much back. I did Chase's taxes, and he got back $1,120. February 23, 2001 was the closing date. For some reason, the date was delayed. We had $2500, plus $1120, plus the money we saved from our checks which was $2300. Added together totaled $5920. I was glad it got delayed. We didn't have enough money yet, so I informed my agent about it. The real estate owner asked, "How much more do you need?". I said, "$2580". She said, "We give a gift to all our customers when they buy a house with us". She wrote a check and said, "Take this to the bank, cash it, then put it in your account. You must put in cash into your account, no check". I did what she told us to do. March 9, 2001, we bought the house. God was in control in all that took place. I couldn't get the house I originally wanted because He had already chosen this one for me. I couldn't get the house without Chase. That brought us back together. We didn't have enough money. He used the owner of the real estate company to give us what we needed.

God is great, magnificent, and awesome. Knowing things are not an accident. There are no words that can explain what I feel now. My faith has gotten greater than ever. In Jesus Name, Amen.

My boss moved me to another department posting money to patient accounts. We were getting another computer program in the office, and in the doctor offices. Once I learned the system, my boss had me train people. Then, he sent me to doctor's offices to train. One doctor's office requested that I come to train them. This doctor was my personal doctor. I didn't do the billing for the office, but I knew the person who did. It was nice because I lived about five miles from the office, and I didn't have to fight traffic. My training took about a month. I returned back to my office. I had been there for two years, and I never got a raise. I went talk with my manager about my raise. She said my annual evaluation hadn't come up yet. I talked to her boss. He said, "How much are you looking for?" I said, "A dollar more per hour. I get insurance with my husband's job, so you don't have pay my insurance". He said, "I don't know if we can give you that much". I asked, "How much, then?" He told me 50 cents. I said, "As much as I do?" He said., "No one ever gets anything higher than 50 cents". The next day, I started looking for another job. About a week later, I had an interview with diagnostic center. They wanted to start me at $12 an hour. While waiting on my back-ground check, I went to work, and put in my two-week notice. A couple days later, the boss calls me in his office with his boss. He asked, "How much are you going to make there?" I told him $12 an hour. He said, "We could give you $11". I said, "you said all you could give me was 50 cents more. Now, you want to give me $11 dollars? Thank you, but it's time for me to go. God always comes first in my life. I know if I keep Him first, all my needs will be met.

Diagnostic Center was a big company where I could grow. I started in collecting, then went to billing. I was able to communicate more with patients. I trained about two weeks. There were four of us working in the billing office. I was friendly with all my patients. After a while, my co-workers thought my phone calls were personal. So, they had the supervisor eavesdrop on me every day. My supervisor, Marissa, seemed to be a little intimidated by me. She was nervous when I came around her. I didn't understand why because she was my boss. It seemed like she felt she had no authority. I asked her if she believed in God. She said, "Yes, I go to church, and I'm in the choir". I said, "You're so quiet. I wouldn't put you as a person who sings". The front desk girl's name was Heather. She was very young. One day, I asked her if she was saved. She said, "I think so". I asked, "Do you believe that God raised Jesus from the dead? The Bible says, if you confess with your mouth, believe in your heart, then you are saved. Heather, do you believe that?". She said, "Yes, I think so". I said in my mind, "I need to help her". We talked daily at work. She told me in one of our conversations that she read the book of Esther. "I'm going to call you Esther", she said. I said, "Okay". I went to read the book of Esther. Esther was a queen in an empire that God used for His people. I thought, "Wow! She read that and thought of me". I had never put myself so high. I thanked her for thinking so highly of me. I said, "I'm here to help you get to be the queen you are in God". She said, "The ladies in the back talk about you so bad. I know you're not like that. They call you a name I don't like". I said, "That's okay. God is going to fix it". Day after day, I committed myself to helping her to get closer to God. I didn't know why it was such an urgency to get her where she needed to be. The ladies in the office would get quiet when I walked in. I would start calling my patients. As soon as I started, my supervisor would come in our office to see who I was talking to. Chase would come and bring roses, and we would go to lunch.

When I'd get back from lunch, I'd see my co- workers talking. They would ask me about my lunch, and say how I'm so lucky to have a husband who takes me to lunch and bring me roses.

I had been there for two years at this time. It was time for our raises. The first year, no one got a raise. My supervisor called me into her office. It's been two years, and she's still nervous when she talked to me. She explained the way they give raises. After she explained every page of the raise book, she said, "Because of all your personal calls, I can only give you a 3% raise". I said, "I don't get personnel calls while I'm working in the office.

I'm talking to patients". She said, "You can write your comments at the bottom of the page". I said, "I don't have any comments". I walked out thinking, "I said I don't have personal calls while working". A couple of days later, I got a new co- worker who worked part-time. She was a student at the university. We became friends the first day. I had trained her. A year later, I began posting payments, reconciling payments at the end of the month on top of collecting for three diagnostic centers. I trained Summer to help me. The other co-worker only worked on miscellaneous stuff. I would get to work before them, and leave after them. I often thought my supervisor was treating me like a slave. When everyone else would leave, I'd turn up the music and Summer and I would have fun while working.

Chase was working overtime all the time at the post office. He said he wanted to make over $100,000 that year. He had worked at every post office in Baton Rouge and surrounding areas.

Chase always had a problem with the supervisors at every office. I told him I thought the reason for him having disagreements with supervisors was, maybe, because he was meant to be a man of authority in Christ. I said, "You need to be a supervisor, then you'd know what to do when you get an employee like yourself". He said, "I don't want to be a supervisor. They can't make the money I'm about to make. I'll be making more money than you". I said, "Working the way you're working, I hope so. What are you going to do with that money?". He said, "I want another truck". I said, "You don't have to make a lot of money to get a new truck. We can get a truck right now". He said, "My credit's not good enough for a new truck". I said, "Let's go see". He said, "Faith, I don't have the money yet". I told him it was okay. We went to Gerry Lane. He picked out a truck, but it was used. I said, "Chase, you already have a used truck you can't fix. Why do you want another one?". He said, "This one I like is good. It has rims on it already. Everything looks good". I said, "Madea said everything that looks good is no good for you. Chase, you always want to get something used. How about this time trying something new?" I went in for a credit check. The salesman said, "It's going to be hard to get the truck you want.

After looking at your credit, why don't you try this new truck?". Chase asked, "Have you been talking to my wife?". He said, "No. I believe you will get this new truck". Chase said, "I can't afford a new truck". The salesman went to talk to the accounting office. He came back and said, "Pick out a new truck. If you get a used truck, your note will be about $500. A new one will be about the same". Chase went pick out a new truck. The salesman asked, "How much can you put down?". I said, "I can write you a check for $1000 if you hold it till next Friday". The salesman looks at me and says, "Yes, we can hold that check. There is something about you I can't explain". The salesman was an older man, so I knew he wasn't coming on to me. It was some other reason. Chase took the truck home that day. He couldn't believe what happened. He said, "You always get what you want". I said, "God says you can have what you want if you only believe. I am asking God for a Mercedes". Chase said, "You're not getting a Mercedes". I said, "Why I can't have what I want? You got what you wanted". The next day, I went back to the car dealer to get the floor mats. Our salesman looked at me and said, "I see the Glory of God on you.

God's Glory is so beautiful on you". I said, "I don't need to ask you if you're saved". He said he's been saved over thirty years. He said, "Your credit score wasn't high enough to get that truck, but God stepped in and made credit no option. You are very blessed". As I left the dealership, I prayed to God all the way home. Lord, I do not want to work at Diagnostic Center anymore. I know I should help the front desk co-worker and I will. God, I am in need some peace. Help me to hold on. God said to me, "Apologize to Marissa." Why Lord? I did not do her anything. She sleeps with my husband, Lord.

Later that day, I realized I called that girl everything, but a child of God. God was letting me know she was His child. God told me this on a Monday. On Thursday, I told Chase God said we should apologize to Marissa. Chase said, "Okay, I know God did say "y'all" because He was talking to me, too". I accidentally answered Chase's phone. It was Marissa. I said, "God told me to tell you I'm sorry. I'm sorry". She said, "Okay, but put Chase on the phone". I gave Chase the phone. I was relieved. Sunday, I typed up a letter of resignation, so I could give my two weeks' notice. Monday morning when I got to work, I went to the manager's office to give her my two-week notice. A manager from the other office was there. My manager asked me when I walked in the door, "How would you like to work in our other office? You'll be working at the front desk with the same pay, and you can get overtime". I said, "I would love that". She said, "You can start Monday". I said, "My vacation starts Monday". She said, "Okay, start the week after". She asked me if I wanted to tell her something. I said, "No, it was nothing". I walked out of that office and tore up the paper. I thanked God I didn't have to look for another job. I was going to get paid the same pay doing less work. I went tell the front desk girl that I was moving to the other office. She was happy.

She said, "I'm going to miss my Esther". I said, "I'm just a phone call away". Chase came in to take me to lunch. He was driving a fully loaded Honda Accord. He said, "This is for you". I said, "Take it back. I don't want it". My co-worker said, "Why did you make him take it back?". I said, "Because I want a Mercedes. He doesn't want me to get it.

God is going to help me get one, and God is going to pay for it." One co-worker said, "That's mean". I said, "I believe, and will receive my car from God".

Two weeks later, I started at the other diagnostic center. It was different there. I was like an older lady working there with college students. They trained me well. Answering and transferring calls was easy. I was the appointment setter. That was difficult to time an MRI and CT scan, but I got it. I met all the ladies there. We talked a little to get to know each other. One the girls said, "I heard your husband bought you a car, and you made him take it back. Why did you make him do that?". I said, "Because everything he asks me for or wants, I get it for him, sometimes even better than he expected. He told me he wanted a truck. I went and got it in my name. I told my husband I wanted a Mercedes. He got that Honda because that's what he wants me to have. That's why I gave it back". One of the girls said, "You go girl. Another said, "I thought you were a witch. I'm sorry", I said, "It's okay. I have been called worse". Shortly after, I got a phone call. It was the front desk girl from the other diagnostic center. She was crying. I asked her, "What's wrong? Where are you? Are you at work?". She said, "No, I'm not at work today. I said, "Please tell me what's wrong". She said, "Nothing bad. I went to church yesterday. I got saved again. I felt the presence of the Lord. I just want to thank you". I was overwhelmed with joy. She got God! It was better than me getting this job. I felt God truly used me to help her. God made me realize that every job He gave me was for someone there. I didn't understand until that moment why I didn't stay at a job long enough to retire. It's because it wasn't God's plan for me.

After the call, the Brown delivery man came to the building. He was very handsome. He walked up to me. I wanted to say to him, "What can Brown do for me?", but I just introduced myself. He introduced himself, and I was in love. I asked him was there anything I needed to get for him. He said, "I just need a signer". He laughed as he walked away. I was serious. I was reading a book called "The Divine Revelation of Hell". I started reading it the night before. This book was the only book I wanted to complete. I usually looked at the table of contents, then find a chapter I wanted, and read it. Not this book. I felt what the writer felt. I smelled what she smelled. I couldn't put the book down. One of the techs saw me reading it. She asked if she could read it when I was done. I asked her if she believed in God. She said, "I don't know". I said, "I'll bring it to you when I'm done. After you read it, we'll talk". A patient came to check in. I remembered her from the other diagnostic center. She wanted me to sit with her as she got an MRI. She was afraid. She reminded me that I went with her the last time. So, I went with her again. She did well. She didn't even move. The MRI tech asked me if I would sit with other patients when they needed it. I told her I would when she needed me to. Weeks later, Marissa called me at my job. She asked had I seen Chase. I said, "What? Why would you call me on my job to ask me where's my husband?". She said, "He calls me every day. He's mad at me. He didn't call me today". I said, "Are you out of your mind?". I hung up the phone, and called Chase. I told him that Marissa called my job. He said, "What she wanted?". I said, "Chase, it doesn't matter want she wanted. She shouldn't be calling my job for nothing. I can't believe you asked me what she wanted". I hung up the phone in his face. I was so mad. I left work, and went home early. When I got home, Chase wasn't there yet. I went bathe. I needed to calm down. A hot bath usually helped.

While in the tub. I began praying. I said, "God, here I am again. I do not know what to talk to you about. I'm so mad that she called my job. I don't know why I got to go through this with this woman. Why should she be a problem in my marriage? I know Chase cares about her so much.

You hear him telling me how she let him have his way with her anytime and anyway he wants. Lord, why me? Why do I have to endure this race I am in? Lord, I need your help on how to do this. Lord help. Why he cannot live here only and just be with me? I do everything You ask me to do. I go where you tell me. Please Lord, help me".

Chase got home very late. I asked him where he was. He said, "At Marissa's house". I said, "What time you got off?". He said, "5:00pm". I said, "Chase, it's 11:45pm. What were you doing over there?". He said, "Faith, Marissa is the mother of my children. I'll never stop loving her or wanting to be with her. She gives it to me when and how I want it. You don't do the things she does". I said, "Chase, we have it at least four times a week. Why do you stay here with me if you want to live that way? Please leave me! Let me go, please, please! You said you didn't want to live in the hood. That's where she lives and who she is". Chase said, "I want to live where ever she's at". I said, "Please go, and be with her. Let me go, so we can move on. After we argued about two hours, Chase left. I went to my bedroom. I called God. *Lord, please make him stay away from me. Lord, I need him to stay away from me for my peace. I need not to worry about this marriage. I know in the Bible you said don't worry in Matt 6. I know you take care of everything. Please take care of Chase and his decisions he makes, but he is hurting me so much. He talks to me like I'm nothing. He belittles me. I know he cannot possibly think of me that way. When I realized he was the guy you wanted me to marry, I didn't see this part of him. Help me Lord to endure this race.*

6:00am, Chase came back home. I was sleeping. I heard the door, and I woke up. He came in, took a shower, then got ready for work. He was gone at 7:00am. I got out of bed, and got ready for work. He didn't call all day, and I didn't call him. This went on for about three days. Finally, he called and asked if I wanted to meet him for lunch. He said he was sorry, and that Marissa should have never called my job. He said he talked to her about it, and it shouldn't happen again. I asked, "Why don't you go be with her?". He said, "Faith, I love you.

We're supposed to be together. I'm not going to be with Marissa. You are who I want". I said, "What I said to you the other night, I was mad. I asked you. You didn't have a reason to be mad at me. You hurt me so bad with what you said. I can't believe you said that". "Faith, I was just mad. I don't understand what you were mad at. Maybe, because you asked what was I doing at Marissa's house. I don't know, but I know I'm sorry". We ordered lunch. He ate, and we got ready to go back to work. He asked me, "Why you didn't eat? If you wanted something else, why you didn't order it?". I said, "I'll take it, and maybe eat it later.

The delivery man came with a delivery. He was the best thing that happened to me that week. He stopped to talk to me for a minute. We talked about his little girl that he adored. He said, "When I get home, she's my conversation that I need every day". I asked about his wife. He said, "She doesn't talk as much as my daughter. I guess she is always too tired". I said, "To talk to you? As fine as you are? I'd have your dinner ready to sit down and talk to you after work". He said, "It used to be that way". I asked him, "What did you do?". He said, "Nothing. I think after the children came, everything changed. I got to go. I'll talk to you later". I said, "Okay. I can't wait for later". He laughed on his way out. One of the techs came up to me. She said, "That's a good-looking man". I said, "He's mine, all mine. I don't want you to even look at him". My co-workers laughed. One said, "I knew him first". I said, "I don't care! I want him all to myself". One asked if I finished the book. I said, "Yes, here it is. Are you saved yet?" She said, "No". I said, "Okay. Read the book and get back to me.

Chase and I were not the same after he told me he loved Marissa and he'd always love her. Our house was never the same. He talked to me like I was one of his boys, as if what he said to me would not hurt. I know sometimes we'd talk as though we were boys, but this time, it felt like he wanted to hurt me. He cut me deep. Deeper than I could ever imagine. The trust is gone. I had no more trust in Chase. He came in with roses, and asked if I wanted to go get something to eat. I said, "Later.

I'm not hungry right now". He said, "I'm going to get fast food". I said, "Just get me a large fry". We talked more about what I was feeling about Marissa. He compared him and Marissa with me and Johnny. I said, "No! It's not the same. Johnny would never disrespect you. He wouldn't call you on your job. I love him, but I wouldn't let him disrespect you. The love I have for him is love. You and Marissa, it seems like you have lust, because if either one of you loved each other, you wouldn't disrespect your children by being together while you are married to someone else. That's giving them hope that you will be together. Johnny and I would cherish our children and respect them. You know how much I want a baby. I wouldn't disrespect our child, ever, and I wouldn't let you disrespect our child. You can't compare the love I have for Johnny with the kind of love you have for Marissa. To me, what you have, is not love. If you let me, I will teach you how to love". He said, "Faith, I don't need you to teach me love. I know how to love. Don't I get you whatever you want and more?". I said, "My kind of love, don't cost nothing. It 100% free all the time. Let me know when you're ready to experience it".

Home Bible Study

The next day, I called my friend Diana. We worked together in 1996 at a tax company. She's ten years older than me with ten more years of wisdom. I know she loves the Lord just as much as me. I asked her if she would like to have Bible study at my house. She said she would, so we did it. We started a Bible study every Wednesday. We took turns heading the studies. We got my sisters, her daughters, our friends, and more family members to come. We had a great time. On one of my Wednesdays, I talked about how it was impossible to please God without faith. I explained how much faith I have in God. I told them, in 2001, I saw a Mercedes that I liked. I had the money to get it, but I was waiting on God to say it was okay to get it. I continued saving my money, but the Bible says, "Faith without works is dead." That means you must do something to prove to God you're serious about what you want. I believed with everything inside of me that God was going to make it happen.

Diana and I was talking. I said, "I don't know what's my gift from God. I can do a lot of things. I sew, cook, paint, decorate, cut hair, fix light fixtures, and do accounting. I needed to know.

Diana said, "I know what your gift is". I said "What?". She said, "You have the gift of Faith". I said, "That's not a gift. Everybody has that". She said, "Everyone has a level of faith, but I don't know anyone who has the level you have". I said, "Okay, I'm going look it up in the Bible". In 1 Corinthians, Chapter 12, it talks about all spiritual gifts. "Faith" is a gift from God. I love it! I have the gift of "Faith". The gift of "Faith" goes along with healing and miracle powers. I remember when God told me I was a healing minister. Now, it all made sense. I must have faith to believe any and everything God says. Whenever God wants me to do it, I will. I am sure I will be equipped to do so.

I began to pray for a baby girl. When I prayed for a son, Chase gave him to Marissa. That was the worst pain in my life. I remember I couldn't breathe. Now, I'm still living with that pain. Every time Chase brings up her name, I hurt. I don't want to go through that again. I began praying with my eyes closed. September 2003. I heard God say, "Open your eyes." I opened my eyes. God said, "This is your son". He showed me a baby. I said, "Thank you God for answering my prayer". The baby was so pretty, I thought it was a girl. I remember sleeping with all these men. So, it was possible my baby would be that pretty. I called Chase at work to tell him what God showed me. Chase said, "Finally, you're going to get your baby". I got out of my bed, and went shopping. I started buying clothes for my son. I also started looking for good schools. I opened a bank account for the baby. I wanted his name to be "Chase Alexander Scott". I was so excited! I called my sister and Vera to tell them what God said. Vera brought over some cloth diapers and some rubber bottoms. She was old school. I wasn't going to wash diapers.

I remember doing that with Fredrick and Kim when they were babies. I'm glad we had disposable diapers. I didn't know how long it was going to be, but I was going to be ready. I started living as if my son was already born. Days turned into weeks, weeks turned into months, months turned into years. It is now 2005. I went to the doctor and asked to be tested. She tested me, and it turned out that my tubes were blocked. My doctor gave me the number to a specialist. I made an appointment with him. He said he could unblock my tubes, if God was willing. I was very happy to know this doctor had faith in my God. He scheduled my surgery. I asked Chase if would he take me. He didn't answer me, so I drove myself. About an hour later, Vera and my sister showed up. I was glad she came in order to get my car home. Chase arrived right before I went into surgery. He asked, "Where's your car keys?". I said, "Vera's going to take care of my car". He said, "Okay". I knew he was up to something. He didn't want me to have that car. I felt like he was going to do something to it. The surgery was over. The doctor said he couldn't open my tubes. There were other problems, but I was under too long already.

A Marriage Money Challenge

March 24th was our anniversary. We took time off from work to go to Virginia to see his daughter.

The day before we left, we were talking about going to dinner at Olive Garden, which is my favorite place to eat. That day, Chase and I decided to refinance the house. After paying all the bills, we had $14,000 left. I said, "Let's save this money for upgrades or other things we need for the house". Chase wanted to buy another motorcycle. I said, "Chase, the motorcycle is $10,000". He said, "I know. You can have the rest of the money for whatever you want". I wanted to save all of it. He got mad. We started arguing about how much he works to get what he wants. We left the restaurant and went home. We argued so much that night.

Chase began packing his clothes to leave. I said, "Chase, everything is not about you". He left.

The next day, I brought Diana to the doctor. Her appointment was for 3:00pm. We got there about 2:45. It was a beautiful day, so I sat outside on a bench under the tree while waiting for her. I heard God say, "Go get Chase", then God gave me a vision showing me where Chase was, and the way the truck was parked. I said to God, "I don't want to go get him, Lord. You saw what he did, and heard what he said to me. Why do I have to go get him? I know he's at Marissa's house. I don't know where she lives. I don't want to go there". Diana came out. I asked her how it went. She said, "I have a little blood problem, but I got some medicine to take care of it. Everything will be okay". I said, "Okay let's go buy some shoes".

Diana asked me if I had been to a certain shoe store. I said, "No, but where is it?" We went to the shoe store. When we walked in, a sales lady came up to us asking if she could help us find anything. I told her I was looking for certain pair of shoes. She said, "You are very rich", then begins to prophesy to me. She told me that my husband was cheating on me, but he loved me. She said I should be careful about the other man that I loved because I could lose them both. I was amazed at what she said. She asked me for my phone number, so I gave it to her. There was a man there who came up to talk to her about something. I said, "Is that your husband?". She said, "I rebuke that in the name of Jesus". I said, "Okay, but that is your husband".

Diana walked over to tell me she couldn't find her size, so she was ready to go. We left.

I took Diana home, then I went home. It was about 7:00 pm. I took a bath, and took a half bottle of cold syrup so I could sleep. I watched two movies. I didn't go to sleep. It was about 12:00 am, so I got up and went to the shopping center. I said to myself, "If he wants to buy a motorcycle, I'll show him". I walked in the store and bought a lawn mower. I couldn't fit it in my car, so I brought it back and bought a weed eater and other lawn gear, towels, and other stuff for the house instead. I spent about $300. When I got home, I heard God say, "Go get Chase". I said, "God, it's 3:00am. He's asleep. I picked up the phone and called Marissa's house. I said, "I need to speak to Chase". She gave him the phone. I told him God had said for him to come home. He said, "Okay". An hour later, I called back. Marissa answered the phone. I said, "Let me speak to Chase". She said, "He doesn't want to talk to you". I said,

"Well, I guess I have to come over there". She said, "Come on". I hung up the phone. I put on my battle clothes, got in my car, and drove off. I had never been to the girl's house. I don't know how I got there. I saw Chase's truck parked the way God showed me earlier. I knocked on the door. I heard Chase say, "Don't go to the door. She has a gun". I said "Chase, you know I don't have a gun. You need to come out so we can talk". He told me to go away. I heard a lady calling me. She lived next door to Marissa. She said, "Baby, you better go or you're going to get hurt". I told that lady, "God sent me here. No one is going to hurt me". It was now about 5:00am. It looked like everyone in the neighborhood was outside. I said, "Y'all, don't call the police on me for disturbing the peace. It rolled to 7:15am. I said, "Chase, you should come out now". He came out, and he saw that his window was broken on his truck. He asked me, "Why you broke my window?". I said, "Now, why would I do that? I need to talk to you". We got in my car and went to a fast-food restaurant. We fussed and cussed.

Finally, we came to an agreement. I took him back to get his truck. I went home. I heard God say, "Chase is going to die". I told Chase what God told me when he got home. He didn't have any reaction to what God told me. That evening, we went out to eat. Chase got a call from one of his friends that happened to be a pastor. He said, "I'm calling to check on you. I had a vision last night that you were going to die". I heard Chase say, "No man, I'm not going to die. I was somewhere I didn't need to be, but Faith came and reminded me where I belong. Thanks, pastor, for calling me. I needed to hear that".

Chase asked me if I had talked to the pastor about what God had said to me. I told him I hadn't spoken to that pastor since the week before. I asked him what he said. Chase said, "I was supposed to die last night". Chase looks so scared. I said, "Friday, God told me to come get you. I didn't want to because I knew you were with her. I don't know why God told me to go get you, but He always knows what's going to happen. I don't know what you were doing. The lady next door to Marissa, told me to go home before I get hurt. I told her God told me to come here, so I must stay until I get my husband. I'm not going to get hurt".

Chase said, "Marissa's boyfriend's mother stays next door". I was shocked. I said, "She has a boyfriend, and you stayed there? That man was going to kill you. You need to stay away from that girl. I don't know what it's going to take for you to stop and pay attention to what is going on in your life. Chase, you take lots of chances. One day, your luck is going to run out. What are you going to do with yourself?". Chase said, "Faith, lets pray". I said, "You must repent and ask God to keep you.

This is not a one-time thing. It has to be for life. You must decide. You can't stay lukewarm, and say you trust God. This is for real". He said, "Okay, I hope God gives me a little time". I said, "Tomorrow is not promised to anyone".

The next day, we went to put a down payment on my Mercedes. Chase's friend came by in his new Honda S2000. Chase loved that car. I went to get the S2000 for Chase. I thought if he gets that car, he wouldn't want to drive my Mercedes and abuse it like my Honda Civic. I took the truck and traded it in for the car. On my birthday, two days later, I got my 2004 Mercedes. I told

Chase, "Because I got your car first, I need you to co-sign for my car". Chase went to the Mercedes dealer to sign.

He called me and said, "You got a Mercedes". He said it with amazement. I said, "Chase, I told you I was going to get it. You didn't believe me". He said, "I still don't believe it. How are you going to pay for it?". I said, "God will provide".

Marriage and Money Challenge

Chase made $92,000 that year working a lot of overtime. He bragged about it. I guess no one else at his job made that much money. I made $52,000 with a little overtime. I said, "Why you always have to challenge me? Okay, it's on now. I got God on my side. I will win". The next year, Chase made $110,000. Chase got what he wanted. He said, "Faith, I made more money than you". I said, "Technically, that's not true because half of your money is mine. I made $57,000 + your half of

$55,000, and that totals $112,000. So, I made the most". Chase said, "Whatever, Faith. I was just saying, but you wanted to get technical". I said, "But you got what you wanted, as always. I am very proud of you". Chase said, "I don't think I will make that much next year".

What Is Done in Dark Will Come to Light

My grandmother would say these words: When we don't tell the truth, the truth (God) will tell on you. I learned later; she could discern (Holy Spirit) when someone is lying.

God hates liars. Prov. 6:16-19

Chase told me Marissa was talking about making him pay child support. I said, "You're not going over there or calling her every day". He said, "No, Faith. I'll listen to you. You told me to stop, so I did". I said, "You should've known it was going to happen sooner or later". He said, "Faith, it doesn't matter about her or my kids. If I have you, I'm good. If you leave me, I don't know what I will do, go or be". I said, "Well you should think next time before you want to cheat".

My phone was ringing all day. I answered the phone, they hung up. I checked caller ID. I didn't know the number. They left a message saying, "Call me". It sounded like a little girl. Maybe, it was one of my niece's friends. They stayed with me the week before. Two hours later, the girl calls back. I answered the phone this time. She said, Tell Chase I'll be putting him on child support tomorrow. I told Chase, "This girl said she is going to put you on child support tomorrow". Chase went into the bathroom and closed the door. I said, "She's still on the phone. Do you want to talk to her?". He said, "No, I don't know who that is". I asked the girl if she had a baby for Chase. She said, "Yes, he was with my family at the hospital when I gave birth to our baby girl. Would you like to see her?". I said, "Yes". Chase came out of the bathroom saying, "I don't know who that is Faith". I said, "Get out of my house. Get all your stuff and get out. I don't care where you go. Oh, I guess you can't go to Marissa's. She's also putting you on child support. The hits keep coming. Go to your mama's. She believes everything you say. Chase, when are you going to stop cheating and lying to me? I told you God will always reveal the truth.

Why you can't stop doing wrong? Now, you're not just hurting me and Marissa, you're hurting this girl and her baby. When are you going to stop hurting me? You said you love me, but you keep hurting me. This time, don't forget anything. Take it all. Give me my keys". Chase said, "That's not my baby". I said, "Get out before I cuss you out to no end". Chase took his clothes, and left.

I put on praise and worship songs. I was thinking about what I was going through, again. I don't know which time hurt the worst. I felt darkness again. I didn't know where to go or where I was in this marriage. It seemed to be getting worse. My husband didn't care to be truthful, even with himself. It just kept raining on my relationship. I felt like I was going insane. I had no peace, and was always in pain. I didn't want to run this race with God anymore. It hurt too bad. I had to lay down and cover my ears. The sound of silence was so loud. I couldn't escape this feeling in my head and the suffering, repeatedly. I wanted to be happy. I needed to be happy. I had no true husband, no child, and no family. God knew all I wanted was a happy family. It felt like I couldn't escape this death in my chest. My heart was hurting so bad. I just wanted to die. I begged, "Please Lord, let me come home. I need peace, your peace. Lord, help me! I can't defeat this acne. God, he had another child in our marriage. I prayed for a child, and he gave it to another woman. God, you've got to help. It hurts so bad that I can't have a baby. Why can't I have my own child? You said I'll have what I ask for. You said you'll never leave me nor forsake me! He is making babies with everyone, but me. Why Lord? Why you chose me to bear this cross? Why do I have to go through so much pain? Lord, I am sorry. Please forgive me. I repent. I know you love me, but I don't feel the love right now".

I wanted to kill myself. I set up everything including what I wanted to wear. I got all my insurance papers in order. I got a prescription of Ambient, thirty pills total. I laid everything out. It was about 9:00pm. I got a glass of water and took the pills. At 11:15pm, I heard a knock on my door. It was one of Chase's co-workers. When I opened the door, he asked me what was I doing. I said, "I was in the bed". He said, "Why are you trying to kill yourself?". I said, "How did you know? I'm tired of living here. I want to go home". He said, "This is not the way. It's not time yet". He started to preach. He gave me some scriptures and asked where Chase was. I said, "I put him out. I don't know, and I don't care where he's at". He said, It's 2:2 am. I've got to go home before my wife calls the police. I'm never out this late". I said, "You should call her from here so I can talk to her, and let her know you weren't doing anything wrong". He said, "My wife knows I'm not doing anything wrong. I trust that my God told her. We laughed, then he left. I realized the medicine wasn't working. I took thirty pills, and I'm still awake.

Time passed by. It was about 11:00am. I never got sleepy. I got a call from the pharmacy. They called to let me know the pills they gave me was the wrong prescription. They gave me Placebos. I said, "What is that?". She said, "A sugar pill. It won't help you sleep. The pills will keep you awake". I said, "Okay. Thank You". That is why I didn't sleep.

I began to pray, *"Lord, here I am again in a place of confusion. I have always been here because of the lies from Chase. He keeps coming home to take out the trash on me. I don't want him here, Lord. I don't believe nothing that comes out of his mouth. He looks innocent, but I know he's not. He's trying again to get back in this house. You know we have been talking. He wants me to think he is sincere. but he's not. I know he isn't sorry, because every time I to believe him, but he always let me down. Lord, I do not trust him. Lord, should I take him back because you know he will come back begging forgiveness? God said, "Can you forgive him?". I said, "Yes Lord". God said, "Take him back. I will be with you".*

My House Was Broken Into

The thief come to steal, kill and destroy. John 10:10

Weeks after I put Chase out, I got home to face a break-in. I checked all over, but no one was still there. I called for my dog, and he came to me. I called the police, and then Chase. I started looking to see what was missing. Nothing was taken out of the living room. I went into the kitchen, and my computer was stolen. I went into the utility room, but nothing was taken. I walked into the hall, and the middle door was open. It's never open. I kept the make-up I was selling in there. I walked in, and the room was a mess. All my stored cosmetics were stolen along with all my files and paper work with my client's names and addresses on it. I walked into my bed room, and my jewelry box was gone. I had a brand-new pair of Nike tennis shoes as you walk in the closet door still there. In the closet, everything was still nice and neat. I saw my leather and suede jackets, and a Coach bag were still there. I had about 75 pairs of shoes which four pairs were boots. I noticed that one pair of boots was taken. I had that pair hand-made in Georgia. I knew if I found those boots, I would find the thief because I had those boots specially designed for me. That was the only pair missing. With all the shoes in my closet, they only took that one pair.

Police arrived, and I let them know what was taken. Chase arrived. He asked what was taken. I went back into the kitchen, then realized my special grill was also missing. I told Chase and the policeman the only things stolen belonged to me. I started to think it was someone Chase knew because he was not living here at the time. Maybe Chase wanted to scare me. The door was kicked in, so Chase asked if I wanted him to stay. I said, "No. I called the insurance company. They are sending someone over to fix the door tonight. When the police were done, Chase left. I began cleaning the house while waiting for the insurance rep to get there. As I cleaned, I started praying, and singing to the Lord. I couldn't understand why they would take one pair of shoes. The shoes cost about eighty bucks. I had more expensive shoes and boots in that closet. After the insurance worker fixed the door, I took a bath, got in the bed, and turned on the TV. There was a newsbreak. Police were chasing a man who had killed someone. They said everyone in the area needed to be on alert. As I watched TV for hours, another new break came on.

Police found the guy they were looking for and made an arrest. After the newsbreak, I prayed for an answer from God on who robbed my house. He didn't answer me right then. I fell asleep.

Weeks later, I went to fill up my car with gas for the week. Afterward, God sent me to Shoppers Mart. There was a woman sitting by the door that I had seen before. I said hello to her, then walked in the store. I met up with a lady I saw in church before. God told me to go to her. I asked her if she needed prayer for anything. She said, "Yes. The police arrested my son, but he didn't do it". I heard the Lord say, "He did it." I started praying for her and her son. As I was praying, I heard God say, "They can't walk in your shoes". I continued praying with her. After the prayer, I walked out the store.

The lady sitting at the door was still there. I asked her why was she sitting there. She said, "I need a ride home". God is good. I said, "I'll take you home". While I was driving, all I could think about was what God said to me. The people who broke into my house was trying to still my identity. I couldn't believe someone would want to be like me. I think all they saw was my stuff. If they looked closer, they would see a hurting woman trying to find her way. I'm so glad God has my back and my front. He is always protecting me, and keeping me informed with what is going on in my life. The lady asked if I would take her to get something to eat. I took her to eat, then dropped her off at her house. The distance I needed to go to get her home, I thought I may need to go back to get gas for me to get home. I looked at my gas needle. It didn't move. That's how God always works. Thank you, God, for using me!

Will ever get a break?

Chase called me several days later to tell me he was having a paternity test done on that baby. I said, "I don't care. I feel sorry for you, Chase, because you can't stop lying and face the truth. You know that baby is yours. Stop prolonging things as if it will change. You will have back child support again". The baby was four or five years old at this time. The test was positive. He had to pay back child support for the girl and boy, the two babies he made in our marriage. I prayed for a son, and he gave him to Marissa. I prayed for a daughter, and he gave her to someone else. I asked God, "What have I done so bad that my husband gave my children to other women?".

I asked God, "Should I take Chase back?". God asked me if I could forgive him. I told God I could forgive him. He said, "Take him back". I took him back, and forgave him. Chase always came back and acted as if nothing went wrong in our marriage. I was hurting so bad. I told Chase he hurt me so bad. He said to me, "Nothing hurts you. You never cry nor crack-up". I said, "Is that what you want me to do? Cry or go insane? Chase, you know I've been hurt so bad in my life. Why would I cry? Crying never helped me in my life. It only reminded me that I was hurt. The reason you are doing this to me is because you want to see me cry?". Chase said, "No Faith. I just don't understand how you're so strong". I said, "I don't understand why, myself. Please stop!". Chase apologized to me for his new baby girl, and again for the baby boy. I said, "Does any of this ever hurt you?" Chase said, "Both times I made these babies". I said, "How much did this hurt you? You wanted babies. I remember before we got married, I was sleeping with a lot of men to give me a baby, and you told me you wanted to be the one to give me a baby". He said, "I'm so sorry, Faith, I think I was in more pain than you. I'm sorry". I said to him, "You know when we got married how much I wanted a child and a family. You're pushing me further away from you. I love you, Chase. I do, but why you can't just love me?". He said, "Faith, I do love you. I want to love you the way you want. I should be able to. I am sorry. I'm trying to love you the way you need. I can't help that I come up short. I am very sorry. I want to love you the way you want and need. I'll keep trying. I love you so much. I'm sorry I keep hurting you".

I called the baby girl's mom to come over. When I opened the door, the baby girl reached out to me for me to pick her up. I was surprised, I never saw this baby before that day. It was as if she knew me. I looked at her and said, "This is Chase's child, friendly as can be. Her mother said, "Actually, that's the first time she did this. Chase was not off from work yet. She told me how and when they met. I know she was very young. If I had to guess, I'd say she had to be at least 25 years old. Chase was 34 at the time. In my mind as she was talking. I was thinking, "What happened with us to make him cheat on me with her?". She didn't look like someone I thought he would sleep with. She met Chase after he got back from Atlanta, GA in 2000. Chase started sleeping with her between 2001 and 2002. She said they met when Chase was working at the Government Street Post Office. I said, "I'm glad I answered the phone when you called that day. Why you didn't come by? I saw you already, so I know you know where we live. I didn't have to tell you how to get here". She said, "I've been passing by here looking for Chase.

Then Chase walked in the door. The baby girl ran up to him saying, "Daddy". That messed up my head. This means he has been spending time with the baby for her to know him, and call him daddy. Chase picked up the baby. Chase asked her mother, "Why are you here?". She said, "Your wife wanted to see our baby". I said. "Yes, I did. Chase, you said you didn't know that girl when she called. So, I asked her to come over. It seems there is much more to this story". I thanked the baby's mom for bringing her over. After she left, I told Chase, "She looks like you, just darker. I don't understand why you want to come back to me".

2005, I was sitting at my kitchen table. Chase was in the back bathroom. I opened my Bible to read it, and I heard God say, "You're going to write a book". I said, "God, you know I'm not a writer. I love math and science. I can figure any formula.

Would you like me to make a bomb? Lord, you know what I like. Writing is not my thing. I didn't walk across the graduating stage because I failed English. I can barely pronounce English words correctly. I can't spell. You know I have to ask Chase how to spell words. You make Chase the writer of the family". At that time, Chase ran out of the back bathroom. He said, "I know what your book is called". I said, "You hear Him too?

What's it called?". He said, "Why She Stayed?" I said, "God, you told him. So, Chase, get to writing. You're a reader and a writer. You should know why I stayed". I thought, "Why You didn't tell him to write the book instead of me? Why me, Lord?".

I prayed that God would give me a job to make good money. I had an interview at Rehabilitation Hospital. I got the job in billing making the money I wanted. On a Sunday, after I was at my new job a whole month, Chase and I went to the Strawberry Festival. I began walking, and my feet got numb. I didn't know why. In the past, when I would feel this, I'd just keep walking, then the numbness would go away. We had a good time at the festival. My feet didn't feel better, it got worse. I told Chase to take me to the after-hours clinic. I needed a doctor this time. The doctor couldn't explain what was going on. He said I needed to see a neurologist. He gave me some steroids in hopes the numbness would subside. I took all the steroids. The numbness subsided, but I was getting dizzy like my equilibrium was off. I was so off balanced, I was throwing up, and couldn't stop.

Chase couldn't handle me being sick. He called Kim and Vera to tell them he was taking me to the hospital. I couldn't move the left side my body. I told the doctor I couldn't feel or taste anything on my left side. He checked my eyes and mouth. He said it seemed to be Vertigo with Bell's Palsy. He gave me medicine for both. I took the week off from work. I got well enough to drive, but I was still dizzy. I went to an ENT doctor. He moved my head a certain way, and the dizziness was gone. He said, "We have crystals in our head. The crystal was touching a nerve, and it causes the dizziness". I asked him to marry me. No one else told me this. A month later, the numbness came back. I called the neurologist, and made an appointment. I explained to the doctor what was going on with me. He told me to lay on the table. He told me to raise my shirt. He touched the right side of my stomach. He said, "You have "Multiple Sclerosis (MS)". You are going to need a spinal tap, and a MRI of the brain, cervical, thoracic, and lumbar. Once we have the results, we will go from there". I went to General Hospital to get an MRI and a spinal tap. It was confirmed I had MS. I asked the doctor, "How did that happen?". He said, "You were born with it. This disease mostly happens with my white patients. I've only seen a small amount of black people with MS". I called Chase and told him. I called Vera and told her I had it my whole life. She said, "When you were young, I remember you said your back would hurt, and you couldn't move. I didn't know. Doctors didn't know either. Maybe, when I was young, the doctors didn't know black people could have MS. Now, I know why I was in pain, and sometimes I couldn't walk or even move. When I got home, I prayed, *"Lord, thank you for letting me know what I got. Lord, I ask that You heal my body. You said ask and it will be given. You said, seek and you will find. Well Lord, I am a looking for a cure. I know I must go through some things, but you promise You will always be here with me. Lord, help me to endure this race with my body and my marriage. I pray this in Jesus Name"*. I learned my faith is big. I know what I know because of God, and God alone. In the book of Ecclesiastes, chapter three speaks of time and change. Solomon, the man of Wisdom, had been through a lot. It reminds us that everything is meaningless without God. So, trust in Him. Don't lean on your own understanding

Chapter 5
God Answer My Prayers

In 2006, God told me to move to Georgia. He said, "Quit you job and sale the house, and go to Georgia". I said, "Lord, I asked you for this house and job.

Now you want me to quit and move?". I wondered why would He want me to quit and move. I waited for days to see if Chase would say something about Georgia. I went to church, and I heard the pastor say, "Sometimes God will take you out and bring you up, then take you back where you came from". I felt at the time God was doing this to teach me something in this move. Weeks after, Chase and I was playing cards. Chase said, "We're supposed to go back to Georgia". I said, "How'd you know? Did God tell you too?". He said, "I think so". We began talking about our stay in Georgia. To me, it was a great learning experience I had from God. I put in a month's notice at my job, and got ready to put the house up for sale. I said, "We should get the roof fixed, and the ceiling in the middle room done, and we did. I went to the realtor that sold us this house. She said, "Yes, I know someone now that wants your house.

Realtors put the house up for sale. A week later, the house was sold. Chase and I went to Georgia to find an apartment. We went to the place where we stayed before, but everything had changed. There were new owners, and the apartment complex went downhill. It used to be nice, quiet and clean, but not anymore. After seven years, everything changed for the worse. We went further down the street. There were some better apartments. They were updated and looked new. We went to their office, and I began talking to the manager. I told her I didn't know how long we'd be there. She said, "You have a contract for one year". I said, okay, but I know God sent us to Georgia, and I don't know how long or why yet". She said, "I know He will tell you". I said, "You know Him. She said, "Yes, I do". I said, "Then we got a lot to talk about".

Chase and I went back to Baton Rouge to finish packing. At the time, we had some things to throw away. I had a dresser that still looked new, so I didn't want to throw it away. While we were outside, we saw a new neighbor moving in. I said, "Maybe they want this dresser". Chase went across the street to introduced himself. Chase said, "We're moving to Georgia, and we have a dresser we don't want to throw away. Would you like it?". The guy came over to help Chase carry it to his house. Chase came back after talking to them, and said, "His wife told me we're not going to be in Georgia long, and we'll be back. I said, " I don't want came back here. I want to start a new chapter in Georgia". We finished packing. I went to get a rental truck, and trailer to haul my car.

When I got to work Monday, I went to talk to my co-worker Vickie. I told her I was quitting, and moving to Georgia. She said, "I'm looking online right now for an apartment in Georgia. I said, "That's great. When are you leaving?". She said, "As soon as I can, maybe January. It will be a new year and a new time for me and my girls. Their dad lives there, so they will be closer to him. I looked online with her. I told her we were moving on the same street where she was looking. She said, "That's where I'm wanting to live". I said, "Great, we can be neighbors. Let me know when everything is final for you and your daughters, so we can get together when you move to Georgia".

My co-workers gave me an awesome going away party. I was close to the hospital administrator. He was a good friend. I told him what God told me to tell him. God had me tell him that he was a pastor. He said his mother told him the same thing, but he wasn't ready. I know God always get what He wants. I told Mr. Jay I never had a boss as kind as he was to his employees. I know he had a call on his life from God. The party was wonderful. I got great gifts. I loved that job. It was a great place to work. Chase said he put in for a transfer. Inside of me, I knew he didn't. I didn't care. I wanted our marriage to be over. I even thought this was it.

This may be God's way of letting me out of this marriage. Suddenly, I got so happy about this move. It would mean no more of Chase's cheating or him worrying about more money all the time.

This could be the best thing ever for me. It could finally be over.

I was on my way to Georgia, and I started praying asking God how was I going to get paid. Instantly, I got a vision. As I was driving. It was like, I wasn't driving anymore. There were so many people just standing in front of me. I heard God say, "2,500". You did an altar call. Lots of people came up for different things, but only one was saved. You just got paid". I was so excited when God showed me that I almost flipped my car. I said, "God, you say go to Georgia and get one person saved. I didn't know who, but I knew I needed to do this. I couldn't wait to get there. I made it to the apartment complex, and went to get my key so I could start unloading my furniture. It took forever. The maintenance man came to check the apartment, and he helped me move the sofa and bed inside. I was so grateful. I thought, "God always has a ram in the brush". He asked if I had cable. I told him I didn't, then he said he would hook it up for me. I said, "Thank you.

Are you saved?". He said, "Yes". He asked if I was going to be living alone. I said, "Yes, for now". He said, "Well, if you need anything else, you know where to find me, no strings attached. I called Chase to let him know I was in the apartment. He asked if I moved all that furniture by myself. I said, "God sent me a ram in the brush". He said, "Okay, be careful". Now, I wait for Monday to come so I can start looking for a job. Maybe that person I need to meet will be at my new job.

Monday came. I looked for a job, but I didn't find anything that day. A week later, I was going to wash my sheets. I saw this young man swinging in the park. I had to walk through the park to get to the laundry mat. When I was done, he was still there. I was focused on getting a job. I was running out of money. The next time I went to wash my sheets, the man was sitting on the swing again. On the way back, the young man was still there. I asked him where he lived. He said, "The apartment over there". I said, "Why are you here?". He said, "I don't know". I said, "Let me pray for you". I don't know what I prayed for with the young man, but when I opened my eyes, he was on the ground. I helped him up. He got up, and thanked me. He walked away, and I went back to my apartment. I thought to myself, "What did I say to him to make him pass out?". I felt so relieved and refreshed. I asked God if that was person I needed to help to be saved, but I didn't get an answer. Wednesday before Easter, I asked God, "What do you want me to do now?". I didn't get an answer. Later that night, Chase called. He told me he is still working on his transfer. I told him how God used me that day. He got a call on the other line, and asked me to hold on. When he came back, he called me Shelly. I didn't say anything. He was talking about the mall. I said, "Chase, this is Faith. "He said, "Oh, I was just saying...". I hung up the phone. He called back all night long, but I didn't answer. I turned the volume on the phone down, and went to sleep. Thursday, I got up, checked my phone. I saw Chase had called twenty times. It was about 9:00am, and he started calling again. About 10:00pm, I got a call from a number in Louisiana I didn't recognize. I answered it. It was Chase calling on someone else's phone. He said, "I'm sorry I called you someone else". I said, "Whatever, I should be used to it". He talked about 10 minutes, then I told him I didn't have anything to say, and I had to go. At 5:10am Good Friday morning, my phone rang. It was Chase. He said, "Open the door". I looked around. I thought I was in Baton Rouge. I heard someone knocking on the door. I opened it, and there he was. He said, "God told me to tell you to come home. I said, "He didn't tell me. I walked away going down my hallway.

Chase followed me. I heard God say, "Submit to your husband". I thought to myself, "I have not seen him for three months. I'll make love to him. I got up hours later to take a bath, and I heard God say again, "Submit to your husband". I said, "God, how much submitting do you want me to do?". I got out the tub to dry my hair. I read the Bible while I sat under the dryer. I opened the Bible to Proverbs 4:13, "Hold firm to instruction; do not let go; Keep her for she is your life." I said. "Chase, I'm coming home". The next day was Easter Sunday. Chase had to leave so he could be at work on Monday. When he left, I laid on the sofa and fell asleep. It was the best sleep ever. I felt like I was floating. I heard God say, "Get up, and read Genesis 22. I said, "This sleep feels so good, Jesus. Can you read it for me?". I got up and picked up the Bible. I turned it to Genesis 22. I heard my voice, but my mouth wasn't moving. Genesis 22 was when God told Abram to sacrifice his son. I felt the presence of the Lord. I couldn't feel the left side of my body. I couldn't move either. It was the greatest feeling ever I never felt from Him before. God read Genesis 22 to me. God said, "Because you did what I asked of you, I will give you everything you asked of me. Go home and get your son".

On Monday, I got a call from Vickie. She said she was coming to Atlanta. I told her she could stay with me. When she got here, we went job hunting together. It was good to have someone to talk to. We went to church on Wednesday night. I told Vickie everything changed since I had moved back to Baton Rouge, then back here. The church in College Park wasn't the same. They didn't have any more Friday night services. I guess it was because the pastor started preaching at a church in New York. We went to the Wednesday service, and it was still awesome. At the end, the minister said there are some women here from out of town.

Vickie and I stood up. The minister asked the church to give us an offering. That was awesome! We didn't ask for money, but we needed money.

God is always on time. Vickie was expecting more money from her daughter's daddy. I was not expecting any money coming in at all. When we were driving home, we both were in amazement for what God had done.

The next day, the pharmacy where Vickie applied for a job called her for an interview. She called to tell me she got the job. I still wasn't working. I applied at a chicken restaurant and a shopping center. I never got a call. Vickie came back from her interview, then wanted to go visit her daughter's dad. We ventured off to find his apartment. I had never been on that side of town before. I had a half tank of gas. I usually have a full tank of gas when I go looking for something. I was so nervous that I would run out of gas. I couldn't find a gas station. The needle got so close to empty, and my fear of running out of gas kicked in. I finally found a gas station. Vickie was happy because I was getting on her nerves with my doubt. We found the apartment, and I dropped her off.

While she was visiting, I went to my favorite restaurant. I ordered my food, and began meditating on God. I was asking Him where I would be living when I go back home. He said, "Go back to your house". I said, "The house was sold". He didn't answer me. I went pick up Vickie, then headed to my apartment. I started packing. I told Vickie I had to go back home. She said, "Where are you going to live?". I said, "God told me to go back to my house". The next day, I called the realtor. She said the people that was going to buy the house didn't get the loan. I said, "That's all God's doing. I'm on my way back". I went to the apartment manager. I told her I had to move back to Baton Rouge. She said, "Why? Is something wrong?". I said, "No.

God told me to move back into my house". She said, "Being a woman of God, myself, I understand". She pulled my contract, walked over to the shredder, and shredded my contract. She said, "Take as long as you need to get your things out. I said, "It may take two to three weeks". She said, "That's okay. Take as much time as you need. I won't put it up for rent until you bring me the keys". I said, "Thank you Jesus", and I thanked her, also, for being a woman of God. I went back to the apartment to tell Vickie she could stay until I got back to get my things. I told her, "The manager said she won't rent this one out until I bring the keys back. This will give you some time to get an apartment, or just stay here. This apartment is big enough for you and your daughters. You wanted to move to this apartment complex anyway. Maybe, all along, this is God's plan for you. You should ask Him what He wants you to do".

My Return Will Never Be the Same

April 2007, I headed to Baton Rouge. Chase and I had been married twelve years. Twelve is completion. God told me to go get my son. In 2003, God showed me a son. It had been four years. Four is a new beginning. God is so good to me. Something was completed. The completion was when I went to Georgia, and did what God had for me to do. God was testing me. I passed the test. He let me know when He spoke to me in Georgia. My new beginning was my son. I longed for him.

As for my marriage, I didn't know where it is going. Chase was still at his mother's house. He lived there while I was in Georgia. I didn't have any furniture at my house, so I stayed at Vera's house until I could get the money to go get my furniture. As I waited, I went looking for a job. I went back to my old job. I spoke with the supervisor asking her to call me if they need any help. She said, "Not at this time, but she would call me if she needs me". Chase called as I was leaving the job. He asked me to lunch. I accepted. We began talking about that phone call when I was in Atlanta. He said, "Faith, I was talking to Shelly and James a lot when you were gone about the church. I accidentally called you Shelly. I sarcastically said, "Sure you did, Chase". I told Chase what God told me about my son. Chase said, "Let's go over to a fine hotel, and get started. I said, "No! God told me to come get my baby".

Chase said, "Where are you going to get him?" I said, "God told me he will be at the hospital.

That's all I know now. I'm sure He'll give me direction when it is time". Chase asked me if he was out of the dog house, yet. I said, "I must talk to God about our relationship. Right now, I don't want you". Chase said, "Girl, you know you want some of this". We laughed. I said, "I don't trust you. I haven't trusted you since the first time you cheated on me. I have tried to, but every time I see a glimpse of light, you cheat again. Why can't you keep it in your pants? You have given me the disease Trichinosis three times in the last eleven years. Why do you think God wants us together because I don't? Maybe He told you something".

Chase said, "God didn't tell me nothing". I said, "Maybe you're not listening". Chase changed the subject and said, "When are you going to get the furniture?". I said, "God hasn't given me the money yet". Chase had to go back to work. He told me he would call me later.

April 28th, it was my birthday. Evan called asking, "Where are you?". I said, "At Vera's house". He said, "We're waiting on you here at the Kids Party Place for your birthday party". We laughed so hard. I said, "Evan, you're so crazy". I had to inform him I was now thirty-eight years old. He's eight years behind for Kids Party Place. I was supposed to go there when I was thirty. He said, "Oh, okay. So, that's how long it been? I'm sorry. What are you doing today?" I said, "Nothing". He said, "Get everybody together. We're coming over to have crawfish today on your "Big Girl" birthday". I told Vera what Evan planned. Vera asked me to come to her room. She said, "I got a credit card if you want to use it to go get your stuff from Georgia". I said, "Yes, I'd like that. I didn't know how God was going to get my stuff home, but God always knows".

The next weekend, I went to Georgia to get my stuff. Vickie and her daughters helped me load the truck. Vickie was living with her daughter's dad.

So, I took the key back, and thanked the manger for her faithfulness. I got back home, and called Chase to come help me to unload. Chase said, "You know the lights and water are on". I said, "Yes. I called last week to get it turned on". He said, "Faith, you always prepared". I told him you got to always be ready for everything.

Weeks later, I found out my first cousin, Tynnia, had a baby. Tynnia was fifteen years younger than me. I always thought she was pretty. I didn't spend a lot of time with her. As a child, she was spoiled by her mother, my Aunt Martha. Her mother wanted her to have everything. Aunt Martha had six other children. Their father died. Martha wanted Tynnia to have what her other children had at a young age. Tynnia's father died about a year before she had the baby. She couldn't handle that pain. She went to the doctor to get meds for depression, and started taking OxyContin which led to other drugs, then Cocaine. Tynnia was using Cocaine for some time. Before I moved to Georgia, I went visit my Aunt Martha. Tynnia was there fixing her hair. That's when I found out she was pregnant. That was the last time I heard anything about Tynnia until, now. Tynnia went in the hospital and had a baby boy, named him, then left the hospital the next day. The baby was still in the hospital sick. He had cocaine in his system. Six weeks passed. My aunt Martha called me. She said, "Faith, God told me to call you. Tynnia had a baby and left the baby. God said it's your baby". I said, "What? Why would God want me to have a sick baby?". I called Chase to tell him. Chase said, "No. If you take that baby, Martha and all her children is going to be at the house trying to take the baby". I told him, "God did say the baby will be in the hospital". When I finished talking to Chase, I thought, maybe that is my son. I began praying to God for that baby to get well.

I went to the hospital to see the baby. The baby got better, and was sent to child protection. I asked the nurse how I could find him. She gave me a number. I called the child protection office to see the baby. The baby was sent to a foster parent home. The clerk had given me the number to the counselor over the baby's case. I called the counselor, and she arranged for me to see the baby. I called Chase so we could see him together. The baby looked exactly like the baby in the vision God showed me in 2003. I said, "This is my baby. How can I get him?". She said, "You and your husband need to fill out paperwork, then go to classes to be foster parents. I said, "Let's get started". Two months later, a woman from the office came to check my house. She said I needed a fire alarm and a fire extinguisher. She asked me if I was married. I said, "Yes. I've been married for twelve years". She said, "Where is your husband?". I said, "We're separated". She said, "Well we can't give you the baby if you and your husband are not together". I called Chase. I said, "Come home now. Bring everything you own and come home". Chase said, "I'm on my way". I told the lady we were not separated anymore. She started laughing. She said, "Once you finish the classes, you will be a certified foster parent". Chase moved in that night. We had to go to the super market. We saw my cousin Kenny, Tynnia's brother. Kenny asked if we were going to get the baby. I said, "Yes. Chase has reservation about getting the baby because of the fuss we may get from the family". Kenny said, "Don't worry about that. No one else in this family is qualified to get that baby. I know with everything I have, this is your baby, Faith". Chase said, "Okay, that's all I needed to know". The next week, we saw the baby again. He was wrapped in a blanket just the way God showed. I said, "When can I bring him home? The foster parent gave him to me smelling bad, and looking so dirty. His hair even smells dirty. He's so pretty". The worker said, "Because you are his family already, let me see what I can do". We were able to keep him for the weekend because we finished the classes, and were certified. My dream came true. I got my baby. His name was Adonis Santana Lewis. God told me to change his name. Chase and I chose Chase Alexander Scott in 2003. I thought, "I may give birth later to a child from my womb, and name him Chase". Chase chose Sean, and I chose Michael for a middle name. It sounds professional. Sean means "the gracious gift from God". Micheal was an archangel which means "a patron saint of soldiers". I spelled his name "Sean Mychael". I was going to spell it Michael, or Mikkel, but I spelled it Mychael because it was a little different. Sean is now three-month-old. The first night, he didn't sleep at all. I woke up like every hour. I didn't know what was wrong. The next morning, he slept about two hours. I called the counselor to let her know he wasn't sleeping. She said it may be the medicine. So, I checked his medicine. It was liquid Albuterol. I called the hospital to ask a nurse what Albluterol was used for. She said asthma and other breathing defects. I asked, "What are the side effects? Will it cause a baby not to sleep?". She said, "Yes. You must give the correct dose". I told the nurse, Thank you. I called the counselor and told her I didn't want him to go back to the foster parent. I needed to keep him. The counselor said she would see if that was possible, and call me Monday morning to let me know.

CHAPTER 6
My Child Was Born

But those who wait for the Lord, shall renew their strength They shall mount up with wings as Eagles; they shall run, and not be weary; and they shall walk, and not faint. Isaiah 40:31

May 19, 2007, my son was born. August 25, 2007 was the day he was given to me. I was so happy, God said, "I will give you all you ask". I went out the next day to walk my dog. A lady came up to me saying, "You're going to have a baby from your womb". I think it was God working through this woman, but why He didn't tell me this yesterday before I got him? She began praying for me. She introduced herself as my new neighbor. She had a new son, also. We began talking about schools and what kind of friends we wanted for our sons. She lived directly across the street. She's an LPN, and I worked at doctor's offices and hospitals. We had a lot in common. I wasn't working at the time, and it was okay. My baby and I was not lacking for anything. I had everything I needed to be the mother God made me to be. God always knows what to do and what time to do it. I love God so much.

I went to a temp agency to look for a job. I got an interview with a doctor's office. I believe God sent me to him because I told the doctor that interviewed me that he was a minister. He was shocked, and so was I. He said, "My mother said the same thing. Why would God want me? I've done some extremely wrong things in my life". I said, "Just ask for forgiveness, and move on". He said, "My manager is not here today. She usually does the interviews, but I want you to work for me. When she gets back, I'll give you a call". I met with his manager, and she hired me. I told her I was adopting a baby. She said she wanted to see him. Everyone loved him. I put him in the daycare Vera worked at. It wasn't even two miles from my job. The job was fun. The front desk worker and I grew close. God strikes again! She needed help getting a car. God used me to help her build her faith. She said, "I cannot afford a Mercedes". I asked her, "What do you want?". The other lady that worked at the front desk tried to talk her out of getting a new car. I went with her to look for a car. I didn't ask God where we should go first. Three months later, I was fired from that job.

Chase wanted to be a cop. At the time, he was trying to get into a State Trooper camp. He went to take the test, but didn't pass. He told me I didn't need to tell anyone he didn't pass. I said, Chase, I don't care about you not passing, just like I don't care about that dumb motorcycle you are in love with. I know while I was in Georgia, you had someone steal yours, so you can get another one. I told you not to buy a used motorcycle. You don't listen. You think I don't know how things work. I listen to God, and walk where He tells me to go. I know God talks to you. I know he showed you things". He said, "Faith, all I saw was you preaching in a place with a lot of people, like Joyce Meyers". I asked, "Chase, where are you?". He said, "I'm not there". I continued, "I can't understand why you don't believe God put us together". He said, "I know He did. It's the reason why I'm still with you. Maybe He put together just to get Sean". I said, "It can't be just Sean. You put me through so much. It's got to be more". He said, "Faith, God shows me stuff, but not like you, all the time". I said, "Why you don't do what He says?". He said, "I'm not ready". I said, "What will it take for you to get it?". Chase said, "I don't know". I said, "I pray that you wake up and see it's all good, and better than you can imagine".

April 2008 A New Beginning

At the age of thirty-eight, Sean came into my life. Eighteen years I wanted a child. I didn't know it would be this way, or that it would take this long. Biblical eight is associated with the beginning of a new era or that of a new order. At thirty-eight, it had been eighteen years. It's 2008, so that's confirmation. May 19, 2007 was when he was born. At this point, he was with me almost a year. Sean has been one of my greatest blessings I've had in my life.

Chase started staying out late again. His excuse this time was he was working overtime. This time, I don't think it was Marissa. I had Sean now, so it almost didn't matter anymore. I was working on adoption paperwork and going to court at least once a month. Sean couldn't be adopted until both parents agreed to give up their rights. The day came for us to find out about the dad. Sean's father was killed, so we no longer had to wait on his signature. We proceeded with the adoption. April 29, 2008, a day after my birthday, I got my present; Sean Mychael. He was the greatest birthday gift. I thanked God for my miracle. Chase was happy I finally got my baby. He was glad he was a part of it too. Sean's birth certificate says my name as his mother, and Chase's name as his father.

2008, I started working at an insurance company. I worked in the billing department. I always wanted to work at this company for the benefits. Having Sean made benefits more important. God had me telling my story about my marriage, and how I couldn't have children. I was prophesying to a girl one day. I told her we were going to have a black president, then a women president. God was really using me at this job. I got a call from my old boss who was the administrator of a hospital where I worked. He asked me what was I doing for work. I told him I was working at an insurance company.

He said, "A doctor here asked if I know anyone who does medical billing. I told him about you, and how you got more money for the hospital than we'd expected. I told her you even got money that belonged to the hospital for the year before you started working for us. I know you will be good for this job, and you can work from home". I said, "Let me think about it". He gave me her cell phone number. That evening, while giving this offer some thought, I realized Sean wouldn't have to go to daycare. I could be with him 24/7. I called the doctor, and she set up a meeting with me. During the meeting, she explained about her billing condition. I told her I would do her billing after I got off from work at my other job. Three weeks passed, and I put in my two-weeks-notice at the insurance company. The doctor wanted to pay me $20 an hour which was more than my other job. Her billing was connected with the hospital in Plaquemine, LA. It was about forty-five minutes from my house. I continued taking Sean to daycare on the days I had to go to Plaquemine. I loved working from home. I was able to spend time with my son, and work at the same time. I had to go to Plaquemine to pick up some work from Dr. Kevin Dejon's office. He was my new boss, Dr. Terse Dejon's, husband. I was also doing his billing.

Their computer system was connecting to my home computer. Everything was going well until Plaquemine Hospital closed. My boss was bothered because I had quit my job at the insurance company to go to work for her. Her husband offered me a position at his office. I worked there about two months, then a Baton Rouge hospital offered him a contract, and he took it. Dr. Dejon and his full-time workers all moved over to that hospital. I wasn't worried about not having a job. I have God.

It's Time to Walk in My Calling

It was he who gave some to be apostle, some to be prophets, some to be evangelists, and some to be pastors and teachers. Eph. 4:12

An Evangelist is someone who says and does what God says at a certain time. I thought, "I can do that". I don't like to procrastinate with God. God called me to be an Evangelist as a minister of healing in 1999. Healing can be a broad spectrum. I thought maybe He wants me to lay hands-on people by His order, or use me to help heal broken marriages. All I knew at that time, I was ready.

April 28, 2009, I turned forty. I can't find a biblical meaning for the number forty, but it is used 146 times in scriptures. I know Moses was forty when he saw the burning bush. An Angel of the Lord appeared in Exodus 3:1-14. Forty years later, Moses parted the Red Sea. God loves numbers.

Now I realize why I'm an accountant. I always go by numbers most of time.

It's now June. I'm not working, and I have my son Sean. He is impacting my life tremendously. I remember in March of 2007; God told me He would give me everything I asked. In 2002, I worked a lot of overtime. All the women I worked with had children. They couldn't work overtime because they didn't have anyone to keep their children. I asked God then, "When I have children, do I have to work, Lord? I want to take care of my children". God answered my prayer. I'm very independent. Making my own money was a part of my independence, so having no job was going to be a big challenge.

In April, Chase started training to be a Sheriff. He never complained about me not having a job, but I was waiting for him to tell me I needed to get one. He had to know where I was all the time. So, when he is cheating, he didn't know where I was all the time. What he didn't realize was that my life is my son. I can't allow him to make me upset because stress would cause a MS relapse. I couldn't let that happen. I wouldn't be able to move to take care of Sean. I'd give myself a shot once a week to control the disease. I couldn't add more to my pain any more than I must.

I asked God, "Should I get a job?". I began looking in the newspaper to see what was available. God hadn't answered me yet, so I sent out my resume. I got an interview the next day at an after-hours clinic. My sister, Kim, had worked there before. In the interview, the supervisor said, "The only thing is that we can't pay you what you made at your last job". I said, "What are you offering?". "She said, "$16.00 an hour". I said, "Okay".

After working there two months, I heard God say, "Quit the job." I kept working. Thanksgiving morning, Sean had103 degree fever. I took him to the hospital. They tried to get the fever down. I began to pray over him.

The doctor said, "He has pneumonia. We'll need to keep him here. In his hospital room, I was praying asking God to take the fever away for my son. I heard God say, "Quit the job". I asked God, "Can't I work until December?". About two hours later, Sean got up and began talking and jumping around. His fever broke. I said, "Thank you, Jesus". The nurses said that has never happened that quick. I said, "That's all God! He's always does things right on time". We went home the next day.

I got to work on December 2, and was fired. The manager was handing me a card to get a job somewhere else. I said, No, it's not you, it's God". The next day, I asked God What He wanted me to do. He said, "Go to school". I said, "God, you know I don't like school. What school?". He said, "Ministry School". I said, "Okay, but where?". He didn't answer. I began calling ministry schools. I remember Ministry of Love school where I attended classes before. So, I called there to see when classes started. The secretary said it had started already. I said, "It's too late". She said, "You need to talk to the dean". I said, "Okay. What is his name?" She said, "Dean". I thought she was being funny. I said, "What?". She said, "No, really. His name is Dean". She transferred the call to him. I asked if it was too late to start classes. He said, "No. Come in on Tuesday, and we can talk". I walked in his office and began telling him that God told me to go to ministry school. He said, "What took you so long? You're the one He talks to me about. You should've been here at the beginning. I heard from God months ago about you. I'm seeing His Glory on you now". I got scared. I said, "What is the glory telling you?". He laughed. He said, "I see you're going to be a force to be reckoned with". I just smiled and said, "You have to laugh. What do I need to start?" He said, "It's $300 a semester.

Classes are on Saturdays at 9:00am, and Tuesdays at 6:00pm. You can start with $100". I gave him $100. He said, Here's the books you need, and you start Tuesday, December 15th. It will take two years, but when you graduate, you will have an Associate of Divinity". I said, "Okay. I didn't think I was going to be a minister, but God knows what's best for me".

Chase was still in sheriff training. Chase and I was in school at the same time. Chase didn't have classes on Tuesday nights, so he kept Sean on Tuesdays, and my sister kept Sean on Saturdays.

My first test, I failed it. The Dean was my teacher. He tore up my test and said, you must take it again". I was so mad. When I got out of class, I said, "I will not come back to this school". As I was walking to my car, a classmate ran out and said, "Don't quit". I said, "That embarrassed me. I don't want to come back". She said, "What did God tell you to do?". I said, "He's the reason I'm here. He knows I don't like school". She said, "My name is Jackie. You're going to pass the next test with an A+. Come back so you can see". I said, "Okay". The next Tuesday, I made an A+. Jackie became a very good friend. I had no problems after that. I wanted to continue until I completed the assignment God gave me.

Chase was doing good in sheriff training classes. He had other sheriff training he was studying.

Chase was excited. He said, "I always wanted to be a cop". He loved the attention that others gave him. They wanted him to help them study. Chase said, "Now, all I need is my new motorcycle". I said, "Why you just can't drive a cop bicycle? You can get a partner, and y'all can be like the show "Chips". Chase said, "That's funny, Faith. No bicycles, but motorbikes. Yes, I remember those two motorcycle cops. Faith you crazy. You do know I want another Hayabusa, right?". I said, "Chase, just get a cop motorcycle, and leave the Hayabusa for the kids. You know you're getting old". He said, "Faith, you know I got to get it. I will soup it up to make it everything I want it to be. I'll look good on it, and it's going to look good on me". I asked, "How you're going to put Sean on that bike?". He said, "Sean's going to ride with you. I'll ride behind y'all on my bike". I said, "Chase, you stupid!". He said, "Faith, don't hate". I said, "I'm not hating. I want you to have what you want, but let me get some more insurance on you first".

I enjoyed going to school. Every class, I felt closer to God. I started my second year not having a job. I didn't have the money for school, and to take care of Sean like I would like to. I was getting unemployment checks. Chase would always pay bills for the house, food, gas, and even clothes. He would never pay my Mercedes note. He didn't want me to have that car. He never wanted me to have what I really wanted. I wanted a Honda Prelude back in the day, but I got a Honda Civic because Chase said so. I wanted my shoe store, but he didn't want me to have it. I did all the work needed to get the loan. All he had to do was sign, but he wouldn't. We would have had at least two stores by now.

When Sean came into my life, Chase started working less when he found out how much money I really made. I told Chase, "I need money to pay the bills". He said, "You make enough money. I know you've been saving your money. You should pay for everything". I said "Okay". I paid the bills for two months. The third month, Chase said, "I'm sorry. I'll pay the bills. That's my responsibility". He started paying for everything again, except my car note. I thought he was paying my note, but he wasn't. I got a call asking for a three-month payment, but God never let me fall. I got a check from my car insurance company that had only my name on it. I didn't know why. It was enough money to pay off my car. God was working it all out. Chase didn't understand that God was always in control of it all. Chase said, "God always has your back". I said, yes, He does".

Prophet Sean Mychael

I know God gave me a special child. The is very special my son hear from God at a young age. I was blown away.

Sean had, what I thought, a problem speaking. I took him to a Speech Therapist to get him tested. She asked, "What seems to be the problem?" I said, "I read to him, and show him cards of different animals. Sometimes he says the word after me, sometimes he doesn't. I went to observe him at the daycare. The children his age is speaking with sentences. He barely speaks words". She said, "Okay, let's test him. After testing him, she said, "I don't see a problem. Some children can be a little faster than others". I told her I had just wanted to make sure he was okay. She said she would set up some therapy sessions with him. The sessions lasted about six weeks.

March, 2011, Sean was three years old. As I was driving home, I heard Sean say, "Mama, you're going to get a white Tahoe." I slammed the breaks and pulled over. I said, "Baby, you can talk". My mind was blown away. He had been in therapy sessions. Therapist said nothing was wrong with him. I was beginning to think I needed a second opinion. I said, "Sean, mama don't need a new car. This Mercedes is paid for".

The day after his fourth birthday, May 19, 2011, Sean got his first haircut. His hair was too long to start preschool. When I left the barber, I picked up some lunch. As I was driving, a car turned, and hit the backside of my car. He hit me so hard, it pushed my car into another car that was in on- going traffic. My niece, Halie, was with me as well. I turned to check if Sean and Halie were okay. I was happy no one was hurt. While I was waiting for the policeman and the tow truck, I called Chase to see if he would take me to get a rental car. As we waited, I remembered Sean saying I was going to get a white Tahoe. I didn't think I was going to have a wreck to get it.

A month later, the check from the wreck was on its way. Chase and I went to look for a Tahoe. I thought, "I don't have a job. I should get a used one". I never bought a used car before. Chase said, "You don't have to get a used one. I'll pay for the SUV. I have to put it in my name anyway". As we were driving, I heard God say, "Go to Jerry Lane". I said, "Chase, we have to go to Jerry Lane". When we got there, a man standing in front of us was holding keys. He said, "This is for you". I said, "What?". He said, "You came here for a white Tahoe, right?". I said, "Yes". He said, "God told me you were coming". Chase and I looked at each other, and I said, "Wow! My son is a prophet". I told the man my son was only three years old, barely talking, but told me I would be getting a white Tahoe". This was so amazing! God gave me a prophet. To God be the Glory.

June, 2011, my unemployment stopped. I went to the unemployment office to find out why my funds stopped. The clerk stated that I was only supposed to get twenty-six weeks, but I got forty-six weeks. I said, "Glory to God". I needed to pay for one more semester. I needed $300 for school, and $250 for Sean to start Preschool. My friend, Jackie, prophesied where Sean would go to Preschool.

We're not Catholic, but I went and applied as a non-Catholic, and was accepted. We had to pay more because of it, but I got him in. The week before my last semester started, I got a check in the mail for $560 from child support. I didn't know Sean's mama had to pay me child support. God showed up right on time. I got the money for my final semester, and for Sean's school. To God be the Glory! I finished school, but I couldn't graduate until June, 2012. So, I had a loss of time from God being able to show me what my next step was for Him.

Johnny called me. I told him I wanted to see him. He asked if we could meet at Vera's house. We caught up on what was going on in our lives. He was doing good. His new marriage was going well. He even got a new truck. I said, "Johnny, you're looking so good". I asked if he was still using drugs. He said, "I'm not using like I was before. I am doing better". I said, "I'm so happy for you.

Johnny, you look like the man I first met. I love it". He asked, "How do you always look so beautiful? You always keep yourself up and altogether". I said, "I miss you. I miss being someone's number one". He asked, "Chase still don't make you feel like you look?". I said, "Johnny, it's been so long since Chase made me feel anything good. We adopted a son". Johnny looked so surprised. He hugged and kissed me. He said, "You got our baby back". I said, "Yes. Our son looks like you". I showed him some pictures. Johnny said, "Faith, this is how our baby was supposed to look like". I said, "I know! You still call me Faith". Johnny said, "That's your name. I'm looking at our son's skin and his hair. God has finally given you, our son. I'm so glad. It's been over twenty years". I said, "I know. I finally got our son. I don't know what God is doing with me. I don't know if we are supposed to get together, or not. I love you, and that will never change no matter who you are with, or who I am with. I'll always love you. It's amazing how we went through so much, and still come together. I hope this relationship never dies". He hugged me and said, "I'm so proud of you. You have come a long way. I love how you love God.

That gives me hope. I know He will lead you and guide you in all your ways".

May, 2012, Chase graduated at the Sheriff Academy. He is now a Sheriff Deputy. I think the arrogance and cockiness got bigger. What will I do? I know once Chase involves himself in something, he puts his all into it. I know he's going to come home with more to the story. He watches the show "Cops". I know he'll come home with cop stories that he'll write, produce and direct. Watch out Baton Rouge, here he comes! I was proud of his accomplishment. He told me he was going to get a Sheriff car. I said, "I believe you. I pray you get everything you want. I know you're going to get a car soon".

Saturday, June 23, 2012, I graduated with an Associate of Divinity. Pastor prophesied to me, "Now it is your time". At church that Sunday, my pastor asked me, "Are you ready to preach?

There's a conference in August. I'd like it if you'd peach there". I said, "Who told you that I'm ready?". She said, "God". I said, "Did He say Faith?". I heard God say to me, "The name means the same". I told her I was ready. She gave me the information I needed. I called the pastor in charge of the conference and he gave me a list of scriptures to choose from. I chose Joshua 1:1-7. I didn't know why I chose that one. August came around. A couple days before the conference, I didn't feel right. August is my season. God lets me know what's going to happen for me in my season. The good things and the bad things. I hadn't heard from Him yet. The weather was not looking good for the conference. Hurricane Gustav was coming to Baton Rouge. I began praying asking Him what He wanted me to say at the conference. The next day, the conference was cancelled. I was so happy. In my season, God revealed to me I would have a storm in my spiritual life. I thought, "Between one and three years, I'll stay prayed up. Days later, I had a dream early in the morning. Chase was on a white Hayabusa, then I saw it turn over, and no more Chase. I knew Chase was going to die on a motorcycle. I didn't tell anyone. I just prayed for God's strength.

Chase and I were waiting on money to come. I was waiting on taxes that I claimed for Sean's adoption, and Chase was waiting on his money for the Veterans Service. Chase claimed it was for his Costochondritis that was found when he was in the Navy. I teased him for four years because he claimed he had Costochondritis. I told him it was nothing but gas, and all he needed to do was cut the cheese one good time, and his pain would be gone. He said, "Faith, shut up!". I said, "Okay.

When you die, people are going to ask me how you died. I'm going to say, "He finally cut the cheese. It cleaned it all out, and he died".

We were planning to build a house. We started drawing up the plans, and getting things fixed in our house to put it on the market to lease it when our new house was done. We were going to move to Zachary, LA on his mother's property. I love Zachary, and always wanted to live there. I wanted to get new windows for the house we were living in. Chase wanted a Hayabusa. Chase said, Let's bet. If your money comes in first, you pay for the windows. If my money comes it first, I pay for the windows and whatever else you want. My money came in first. I lost the bet, so I paid for the windows. His money came in the same day. I paid for the windows and Chase paid for whatever else I wanted. Then, he asks me to come with him to pick out his Hayabusa. When we got there, the store had two Hayabusa's in the store. A white one, and a black one. I said, "Chase please, please pick the black one. It matches your car". He said, "No, the white one matches the Tahoe. I'll be towing my bike with it. The white will match the truck. I'll soup the bike up to match my truck too. Everybody is going to see my spinning rims". I said, "You stupid! Nobody is going to see the rims spinning while towing it". He said, "No, but they're going to want to see them spin". I said, "Chase I had a dream. I saw you on a white Hayabusa, then I just saw the white Hayabusa. You were gone". He replied, "Faith, I don't care. I'm going to ride till I die".

Months later, Chase was driving his car, and someone in a company truck hit him from behind. Chase called me to come meet him. When I saw the car, the only thing that was wrong with the car was the tipped bumper, but that was from earlier that year. Chase called a lawyer and got paid. It was amazing how an old mishap with the bumper got Chase more than the amount we needed to get the land cleaned up where we wanted to build the house. He paid off the Tahoe. We didn't want to have any old bills with the new house. So, he paid all our bills off. We weren't late on any of them because Chase was always hustling. I loved him for that. He always made sure I had everything I wanted. I remember, every time we broke up, he would get me a makeup gift card and my favorite chocolate candy bar, or one of my favorite male singer's CD. After a big fight, he'd come back with diamonds or some shoes for me. When he got me shoes, that was the best make-up night ever. I realized his goods out- weighted his bad. So, I put my savings in our joint account. We had $70,000 for our new house.

In 2013, it was our eighteenth anniversary. A new beginning. I felt in my spirit that God was directing Chase and I to do marriage counseling in our home. I told Chase what I felt, and he agreed we should talk to people about their marriages so it could possibly help ours. We began our marriage counseling meetings once a month. Chase was helping so many men with their marriages. I was so proud and happy to finally see the ministering side of him. Seven months later, Chase acted like he wasn't interested in the marriage counseling meetings anymore. I heard Chase on the phone talking to someone, saying, "I want to be with you too". I didn't say anything to him about it. At that time, I knew I was growing with God. It didn't bother me as much as it did in the past. I went in prayer. I asked God, "Why did you keep me in this marriage this long?" God said, "For 18 years, I was teaching you how to love the way I love, unconditionally. I said, "Did I pass the test, Lord?". He didn't answer me. We cancelled the meetings.

The Death of a Close Friend

January, 2013, Octavia came by. The night before, I was feeling bad because I took my MS shot. The shot always made me feel bad for hours, sometimes 24-32 hours. Octavia asked, "Where is Sean?". I said, "The MS shot made me sicker than usual. Yesterday, I asked Kim to keep him, so I could get some rest". Octavia looked like something was bothering her. I asked, "Why are you here? You usually call to check if I am home first. I didn't expect you to come today. What going on?". She said, "Nothing. Everything's okay. I'm just tired. I asked her if it was the cancer. I know it had been a difficult time for her, especially the last three years. I told Octavia, "I love you very much! This season with you was a learning one. You taught me how to be bolder, and there's more colors in this world like light gray is not light gray to you. It was revere pewter or dark brown. It had to be carob or hickory. How about chocolate, coffee, and mocha? See, I can pronounce them".

We laughed so hard until we cried. It was like our last laugh. I said, "I thank God for you and how He brought you to me". We talked little bit more, but I was feeling tired. I gave her a hug and kiss. She left, and I got back in bed.

In June, Octavia's daughter called me to let me know Octavia's doctor had just left their house. The doctor said that Octavia had about a week to live. The cancer was in her liver. I called Chase to let him know, then I rushed to Plaquemine.

Hospice was to be there the next day to give medicine to help her with pain. She barely knew who I was. I was there for two days. When I went back Wednesday, June 19, she was gone. She had died the Tuesday night. I didn't know how to handle the news. I knew that day was coming. I should've been more receptive. It could not be stopped with prayer or laying hands on her. It was her time to go. I just had to put it in my head that there was nothing I could have done. She wanted to be cremated. At the memorial service, there were lots of pictures of her. I think the whole town of Plaquemine was there. Octavia had a big fan club. She wasn't a stranger to anyone. She was happy-go-lucky, and always willing to help with any and everything. She could cook, design and decorate. I knew I'd miss her so much. I couldn't cry, I was so happy to have her as my friend. The speaker had everyone laughing by telling the things she did with a happy spirit. It was a great celebration. All I could say was, "Goodbye, Octavia Jackson. I love you".

Time to Preach as An Evangelist

An evangelist preaches where and when God says. And go where God says go you.

After I was supposed to speak at the conference in August of 2012, and I had chosen Joshua 1:1-7, God had given me a vision for that conference, but it was canceled due to the Hurricane Gustav.

August, 2013, there was another conference. I was told I had to speak at this conference to make up for last year. The most awesome thing was that everyone had to preach on Joshua 1:1-6. I was glad because 2014 was coming up, and four is a new beginning. That's what Joshua walked into, his new beginning. The Friday before the conference, my Uncle BoBo died. His funeral was on the conference weekend. I asked God what should I do? God said, "Let the dead bury the dead". It reminded me of when my cousin Floyd died. I was in ministry school, and couldn't miss my finials.

Before Floyd, my cousin Patrick died, I had a finial the same day. I was close to Patrick and really wanted to go. I asked God both times, and each time He said, "Let the dead bury the dead". God always wins with me.

The conference started. There was two men who preached before me. They preached like they were "big time preachers". They had books and computers. I had was my Bible. I wrote some notes on a sheet of paper, but that's all I had. My preacher instructed me it was my turn. She spoke so well about me; I forgot I only had a piece of paper. I walked up, grabbed the mic and said, "Y'all have set me up after the beginners showed up like professional pastors. I wasn't ready for that". They laughed, and I began with a prayer. The Bible says Joshua was about to start his new journey with God. He was to instruct the priest they had to clean up. After cleanup, they were to repent of their sins, then ask God for forgiveness.

They couldn't get close to God, otherwise. I talked about how God gives us the ending of something, and we try to do it our way. We should know God ways are not our ways. God said "I know" twice in the Bible. I talked about the time God told me I was going to have a son, how I was buying clothes, checking out schools, and getting a bank account before I even saw him. Two years passed, and I wasn't pregnant yet. So, I went to the doctor to find out. I found my tube was blocked, and the doctor said he could fix it if God was willing. I told them how the surgery went wrong, and the doctor said he wasn't able to open my tubes. He had to call another doctor because my bowel was tied up with my tube. That was a time when I was going before God said it would happen. I explained Joshua had to let God go before Him, so He could clean the way. At the end of my sermon, I said, "Just wait on God".

Everyone clapped. I was glad they got it. Even the men who preached before me said it was good. I was glad because they had awesome sermons. One of the preachers asked me and the men who preached to meet him for breakfast. I asked, "What time?". She said, "8:00 am". I asked, "Like in the morning?". She laughed, but I was serious. I didn't want to get up that early. I met them and brought my son with me. They asked us three to preach so they could critique us. I didn't know that was why my minister asked me to speak. I remember one of the ministers saying to me, "You had no notes. I said, "Because God was in control". Another minister said, "You only took 13 minutes when everyone else took 22-30 minutes". I said, "I was instructed to take 15 minutes". He said, "Yes, I know". The other minister said, I liked how you put your testimony in your sermon. All in all, you did very well". I said, "That was all God". They handed me a School of Ministry Preaching Clinic Award. The award stated "A certificate of recognition for study, preparation, and preaching to the Glory of God". I was amazed how my pastor didn't prepare me for this. I asked her why. She said she didn't want me to be nervous and worry about it. I was nervous, but I didn't worry.

Hope for a New Home

Chase and I got the plans for our new house. It consisted of four bedrooms, 4 1/2 baths, with living area totaling 3,876 square feet. We had storage, pool, outdoor kitchen, and a three-car garage totaling 5,722 square feet. The house would be too much for me to clean. I'd have to find a housekeeper. For Chase, it was just right, and he wanted a big generator. I started shopping. I got the living room and kitchen table set. Sean's things, we had already. I bought the mattresses for the spare rooms. My bed had to be special because I spend a lot of time sleeping. I didn't want to get the guest bedroom furniture until the house was finished. We had to choose where to build a street on the land so they would know where to put the sewer. I didn't know the sewer goes under the street. Chase wanted to name the street "Scott Lane". Zachary had a street named that already. I said, "Being it's on your mama's land, lets name the street after her. Chase called his mama to tell her I wanted the street named after her. She said, "I don't care what's the name of the street".

Chase had her thinking I was the worst women in the world. This was one of the reasons I didn't want to build on her land. We wouldn't be left alone. If she tried to find out more about me on her own, she would know I am not that bad of a person.

December, 2013, I was getting everything ready for Chase's birthday and Christmas. Chase said he didn't want anything for his birthday, but he said that every year. He really didn't mean it. I bought him a name brand suit for his birthday. He loved it. I got all Sean's Christmas gifts on Black Friday.

That year, Black Friday started on Thanksgiving Day. Chase wanted a Polo Jacket, so I got him that for Christmas. I prepared a romantic Christmas Eve. Every Christmas, he would give me $1000. I would get clothes or jewelry with the money. He surprised me that year. He gave me an open-heart necklace, two bottles of my favorite perfume and

$1000. I was shocked that he physically bought me something. He could've bought just the necklace. I would have been just as happy. I thought he really wanted me to do something special that night. I said, "Why did you do so much for me this year?". He said, "I may not be here next year". I got silent.

I knew our time was short.

God called Chase to be a minister. He told Chase several times by several pastors. Chase wanted to be Chase only. I saw so much goodness in him, even when he did me wrong. I prayed for him so much until I couldn't pray anymore. I remember my pastor telling me to pray for him. I was thinking, "What for? I'm done praying for him. I can't make Chase change and seek God. He must want God for himself. I have shared everything I had with Chase. Time after time he let me down. I gave him all of me until I was no more. I lost my drive, my want to do, and be. I'm tired".

So far, I think I have had enough pain with this man. I cannot take anymore. I trust that God has more for me. I am very lonely. I have been for some years now. I need someone to hold me and make me feel loved. I don't see or feel it in this marriage. I haven't for a long time.

CHAPTER 7
I HAD ENOUGH!

After Christmas, 2013, my sisters, their children, Vera, Sean and I went to Atlanta to spend time with my Aunt Debra. She had cancer. We wanted to bring in the New Year, 2014, with her, her daughter and her grandchildren. My cousin Sheba was there. I told Sheba I wanted to go to College Park church on New Year's Eve to hear the prophecy of the year. Sheba was excited about going. New Year's Eve, I asked if anyone wanted to go with us. No one else wanted to go. Sheba and I headed to church and I began talking. I talked about how many years I was married. I said, "I know God has a plan. I just wish He would let me in on that plan". Sheba talked about her husband. I said, "Maybe, we will get an answer tonight". It started with a comedy show, then praise and worship music. He asked everyone to pray. I began praying about my marriage. I said, "God, I'm tired. I can't go another year in this marriage. I can't take the lying and cheating anymore. Lord, I lost trust in Chase years ago. I don't want to live like this anymore. Lord, I need your help". Sheba and I both had husband problems. I hoped she asked God specifically what she wanted Him to do in her marriage. I prayed we would get what we wanted, and what we needed that year.

A week later, I attended the women's monthly meeting at my church. While waiting for the meeting to begin, Chase sent me some pictures on my phone of his daughters. I text him and said, "They are beautiful". I was sitting by one of the women and showed her the pictures of his daughters. She said, "I didn't know Chase had another child. I thought Sean was the only one". I said, "He didn't want people to know all his business. That's what he told me. I just agreed.

Since the year started, I've taken to all his children". She said, "All his children? How many does he have?". I said, "Six, plus Sean". She said, "WOW!". I said, "I know". I began showing the other ladies the pictures of Chase's daughters. They were shocked because they didn't know Chase had other children. He only talked about Sean. I said, "Yes, he has two other sons and four daughters. He made a son and a daughter in our marriage. The others happened before we got married. Can we start the meeting?". The meeting began. I heard God say to me, "Chase will die this year". I thought, "God heard my prayer". When I said to Him, I can't take this marriage anymore, God showed me Chase was going to die on his motorcycle. Last year, when he had that little wreck on his bike, it must have been a warning for Chase. Chase had it painted a blue color with the Dallas football star on it. He put special lights around it that you could only see at night. It was pretty. He got the bike back and said to me, "Faith, the bike isn't white anymore". I said, "God knows that is the same bike, Chase". Chase said, "I'm going to ride till I die". At the end of the meeting, we always had prayer. I asked for prayers for me to have the strength to endure this race I was given.

When I got home, Chase was looking on the computer for some shoes. He asked me what I thought about a pair he had bought, then he showed me a couple pairs of tennis shoes. I asked, "Why are you buying shoes?". He said, "I always wanted them". I said, "You won't be wearing them where you're going". He said, "I got a little time". When he made that statement, I knew God told him he was going to die soon. I thought, "That's why he bought me that open-heart necklace for Christmas. He knew then. Now, he's rushing to get things done. He told me not to leave from this house. He said, "Don't look for another house, just stay here". I should've realized then, that God revealed to him he is going to die soon".

The next day, after I picked Sean up from school, I bought him a snack and went home. Chase, Sean and I were sitting at the kitchen table. Sean ate his snack, then began his homework. While helping him with his homework, Chase was sitting at the table with the laptop looking at airplane prices. A little while later, my phone rang. Chase looked at my phone and saw Johnny's name. All hell broke loose. Chase and I began arguing. I told Sean to go take a bath. Then it was on. I said, "Chase, I didn't tell him to call me". Chase said, "He should never call you". I asked Chase why he was so intimidated by Johnny. Him and I had been over. The relationship I have with Johnny is, literally, brotherly love. I think of him like Evan and Fredrick. Chase said, "You shouldn't be talking to him". He walks away to the bathroom where Sean was taking a bath. He begins fussing at Sean about the way he was bathing. I heard Chase hit Sean. I got up, went to the bathroom, and asked Chase, "Why you hit him? Is it because your mad at me?

Look at Sean's butt. Why you hit him so hard knowing he's wet? Don't touch him anymore. Get out of this house". Sean was crying so hard, he couldn't breathe. I said, "Breath baby. It's not your fault. Let me help you dry off". Sean said, "I didn't wash my ears and he hit me. Mom, let me wash my ears, then he can come back. I can tell him I'm sorry". Sean began washing his ears. I helped him. I wanted to cry. I thought, "Why you want to hurt my baby? Chase should hit me, not my boy". The next day, Chase came home after work. I was sitting at the kitchen table helping Sean with his homework. Chase walked in bearing gifts. He said, "I'm sorry Sean for hitting you yesterday". Sean said, "It's okay. I forgive you". Then Chase said to me, "I'm sorry. Johnny can call you. You can have anyone you want to call you". I said, "Chase, it's not like that. I don't want Johnny or any other man to call me. I think, because we were having such a good time yesterday, the devil had to put a hand in it. I'm sorry. I just hope you can see that". Chase said, "It's okay. There is a doctor that wants me. I need to give her what she wants". I said, "Okay Chase. Do you, not that you need my permission. You always do what you want to do". Chase left out the house. I knew I wouldn't see him for a couple of days.

January, 2014, Chase heard our first pastor was out of prison. Chase said, "Faith, it happened like you said. The pastor wouldn't do fifteen years in prison. Let's go to Bible study". I said, "Okay". The following Thursday, we went back to our first church. The pastor looked happy to see us. Chase said, "Faith, the church is packed just like you said". I said, "God talks through me. It's not me".

After church, Chase and I introduced Sean to the pastor. The pastor said, "That's a special little boy". I said, "You're right about that. He's very special". Chase was happy to see the pastor doing well. As we were leaving, Chase said, "God always speaks to you". I said, "Because I am always listening. I don't understand how you think so little of me.

God always shows His greatness in me because I'm always looking for Him to show His greatness.

He's always showing you things too, but you just walk away". He said, "Faith, I know how special you are. I've treated you so badly in this marriage. I love you, and I couldn't live without you, including all the times you put me out. I finally realized that I need you to keep me in your life. I thought I needed other women all the time. I don't know why I'm like that". I said, "You like the attention they give you. You love to be noticed. I don't think you truly know how handsome you are. You put on an act as if you know, but I don't think you know. If you don't know, you'll know soon enough. You don't have to be so loud. You wanted to be with those younger girls, and with great and beautiful women. You are a good communicator at every job you've worked at, but you're not a good communicator with me. You want, in every area of your life, to be the most popular. I think this is a part of that "Only Child Syndrome". It's your mama's fault. She should've had more children. I think that's why you have so many children. My grandmother was an only child. She told all her children and grandchildren to have more than one child. It's okay Chase. I love with the greatest love you can imagine. I need to thank God that I have the love now that didn't exist until I married you".

In February, we were preparing for Chase's daughters to come to Baton Rouge for his son's graduation in May. Chase asked me to help him. I got airplane tickets for his daughters. One lived in Virginia, and the other in Florida. Flights were set for May 19th, Sean's birthday. I began getting the house ready. I took the queen size bed out of the middle room and put twin beds. I bought more bath and face towels. I went in our storage room and got more glasses out. It is now March. Every first day of March, I get things ready for our anniversary. This time it was different. I knew this was our last one, so I wanted to make it special. I got a suite at the Hilton. I got some candles, and rose petals. Although we always got a room at a hotel, we never got a suite before, and we never had a romantic setting on our anniversary. I told Chase it was a surprise. Later that week, Chase said, "Let's go get Sean's birthday present". I took Sean to school, then Chase and I went to breakfast. We talked about his daughters coming to stay. He seemed very excited. We were having a very good conversation, until it was time to go shopping. I knew in my heart why he wanted to get Sean's birthday present early. Chase knew his time was winding down, and he wanted to do it, just in case. He always wanted Sean to have the best of everything, so he wanted to get Sean everything he asked for just like it was for him when he was a kid. I think, maybe, he was giving Sean what he didn't give his other children when they were younger. We arrived at the department store. They were out of the game system. I said, "We'll go check at another store". They did have the game system, so we got it and a game. We left there and went to the mall. I got some shoes, as usual, and Chase didn't get anything. He looked like he was worried about something. I asked, "What are you worried about?". He said, "I'm just thinking". I said, "Your thinking looks like it hurts". We laughed, and left the mall. I told Chase I had a great morning. Chase said it was because of the shoes. I said, "Yes, what else? No, it's being with you".

19th ANNIVERSARY

Saturday, March 22, we celebrated our anniversary because March 24 was on a Monday, and Chase would have to take a day off for it. Saturday morning, I took Sean to Kim's, and went to the hotel room to get it ready for that evening. About 3:00pm, I went to a place where they sell love toys, so I could get a pill that gives me the desire for Chase. I wanted to "want him" that night. For about three years, I had no desire for my husband because of all the women he was sleeping with, and still sleeping with. I needed to pray I wouldn't get a disease. I just prayed everything went well. I left the store, and headed home to get his Sheriff uniform for Sunday, and underwear for that night. I took a bath, then called Chase to have him meet me at the hotel for 7:00pm. I called the hotel to order dinner to be brought to the room for 6:30pm. I left the house at 5:30pm to go to the supermarket to get some strawberries, whip chocolate and champagne. We don't drink, but we were going to that night. When I arrived at the hotel, the clerk said, "You look very good". I said, "Tonight, I'm celebrating my 19th wedding anniversary". She said, "We're going to send you some champagne to your room tonight". I said, well, I'll take this bottle back to the supermarket". About 6:35pm, the food was at the door.

Chase called me about 6:47pm to ask me what room I was in. I said, "405". I lit the candles, put music on, and I sprayed my perfume. I had rose pedals spread all over the bed, and from the bed to the door. He knocked on the door. I opened it and said, "Surprise!". He said, "You look so good". He came in and looked around. He was amazed. He said, "Faith, this is a great surprise. I thought you didn't love me anymore". I said, "You're wrong.

I've never stopped loving you". We hugged and kissed. I said, "Now, go take a shower. While he was showering, I made sure the food was still warm. When he got out of the shower, he said, "I don't need food. All I need is you". So, we made love like we did at the beginning of our relationship. It was almost like the first time. We touched each other so passionately. It was the best feeling I had in a long time. I never took the pill. All I needed was the feeling of the first time to get me hot. It lasted a long time like the first time did. It wasn't quick like it had been before that moment. It was beautiful. Later, we got up, ate, and played cards like we did every anniversary. We had champagne and strawberries while playing cards and reminiscing the past. It was a wonderful night. Of course, we had more sex before we fell asleep. When morning came, we talked about how we enjoyed the night before. I mentioned wanting to go to New York for our 20th anniversary. Chase said, "We're not going to have a 20th anniversary, but you can still go with Sean". I said, "It won't to be the same". Chase said, "Our vows are till death do us part". I said, "Yes, till death do us part. I love you, Chase". Chase said, "I love you too". I said, "We should go get breakfast, then come back to our room". We got dressed and we went down for breakfast. Chase didn't want to eat. He said, "I'm going to be late for work". I said, "Okay. I ate breakfast, got my bags, then went home.

For our 18th anniversary, Chase came home with his sheriff uniform on. I thought it was his lunch break. He was in a panic state. I said, "Chase, what's wrong? Somebody died?". He said, "No, worse. I might get fired from both my jobs". I said, "What did you do this time?". He said, "I went to a house where an alarm went off, and it was on my route. While on my way, I saw my co-worker from the post office". I said, "Okay. Why are you going to be fired?". He said, "I was supposed to be at the post office today. I called in. You're not supposed to call in to work to go to another job". I said, "Oh, I see. Chase, you know the rules of the post office and the sheriff office. I can't understand how you can't remember those rules. You know the books on all rules. I don't know why you try to find ways to break them". Chase said, "I think I'm going to be suspended from the sheriff office. I don't know about the post office". I said, "Let's pray". Chase said, "I can't talk to God right now". I said, "Okay. I'll talk to Him on your behalf. Just listen and agree. I began praying, "God forgive us for our sins known and unknown. Thank you, God for giving us this day. I thank you God for your mercy on this situation. Lord, give Chase the wisdom on this mountain he must climb. In Jesus name, Amen".

The next day, Chase came home and said, "I got suspended for thirty days with the sheriff department, and one week without pay with the post office". I said, "That's good, but you have so many days with the sheriff office. It's just a reserve job. The post office is your main job". Chase said, "I know. I have someone in the union to handle that for me. I must return everything that belongs to the sheriff's office. The car, my badge, and my gun. All their stuff must be returned by March 31st. My suspension begins April 1st. I said, "Good. April is my birthday month. My present from you this year is for you to go to Bible study on Thursdays, and church on Sunday. March 31st, I followed Chase to the sheriff office to return the car and all their belongings. Chase was disappointed. He drove us home. He was driving reckless, like he wanted to wreck. I asked him to slow down. Sean said, "Dad, you're scaring me".

He slowed down for a minute, then started back driving crazy. I started praying for me and my son to get home safely. We finally made it home.

Thank you, Jesus! Sean got out, and hugged me.

Thursday, April 3rd, was the first Thursday Chase came to church with Sean and I as a family. It was the first time in years we were together at Bible study. When it was over, pastor announced that we were going to have foot washing the next Thursday. Chase said, "I hope everybody lotion's their feet". Everybody laughed. He told them to use Kari Lotion because it's the best. He said, "I repeat, no one should come with ashy feet next Thursday". I heard somebody say, "Chase, you are so crazy.

Him and Faith are so alike. Faith, please don't forget the lotion for next week". Sunday, April 6th, we were getting ready for church. Chase said, "I finally get to wear a pair of my new shoes. How do I look?". I said, "You look very handsome". He said, "I'm talking about my shoes". I said, "I'm talking about you. I see God's Glory on you, but your shoes look good too". He asked, "You think anyone else will notice?". I said, "If you're walking anywhere, you'll make sure someone notices your shoes". When we got into church, Chase was posing his shoes. He tried to make everyone see his new shoes as if this was his first time with shoes. When we sat down, Chase looked down at his shoes and looked up at me. We couldn't do anything, but laugh. I said, "You stupid fool. Stop showing off in service". I saw a different Chase. I can't explain what I saw. I just knew something was different about this visit to church. Chase was different. All I could see was God's Glory on him. After church, Chase wanted me to drive to go to lunch. When we're together, Chase always drove. As I was driving, I heard Chase praying in other tongues. It was so peaceful in the car. Sean and I were in awe. I knew it was God. I started singing worship songs. Chase wanted fast food. When we got home, Chase wanted to see the game. He had company show up. It was my cousin's husband who came over to talk to Chase. I started cooking dinner. After his company left, we talked a little while, then ate dinner. Chase went in the living room, as usual. He came into the bedroom, and said nothing good was on TV. We watched TV together. He said, "You think I want to have sex, but I don't. I said, "It's been a long time you watched TV with me without a mission". He said, "Yes, I know. He asked me how did I feel. I said, "Wonderful. Today was a great day. Thank you!" He held me so tight. It felt unexplainable, almost unreal, but it was beautiful to me.

Marriage and Changes

Married women are put here to teach each other how to love. I learned when Chase and I had marriage meetings, that you're not in love until you are married. In the beginning of a marriage, you're teaching each other. The weaknesses, strengths, needs, what they like eating, and their dress style.

You find what you need in your mate. You have an opportunity to show each other caring and sharing. It takes time to truly love your mate.

You get married, then you don't like something your mate does. Without praying or asking for help with counseling, you get a divorce. You think you've found love again, and get married. You haven't dealt with the old stuff from the last marriage. Little do you know, the thing you didn't like in the first mate, the new mate has the same problem. Maybe it wasn't your mate with the problem, it was you. God uses other people to help us get closer to Him. God always wants to be a part of our lives. You should take the time and think what went wrong in your old marriage. If you can't see it, God will show you. Before your next marriage, you should really take the time to learn yourself. It may take some time, but it will be worth it.

Jesus is the Bridegroom. Matt 9:15 says Jesus' bride is the church. Marriage is not just for you. It is for the Lord. As a Christian, you must not take marriage for granted. We need to learn how to share, give, receive, and forgive. Forgiveness is huge in a marriage. When you forgive, you are showing love. That's same kind of love God has for you.

Learn to appreciate your mate. I know I learned how to love through this marriage. God showed me "the real me". The one that needed to change. My kind of love was good, but not the best. I needed the best to teach me. In this marriage, I began "love training". I still have a long way to go. It's why I am still here. This love training is not over until God says it is over. The question, "Why she stayed?" is because this was the way God chose to teach me how to love. God made me this way, and made Chase that way, so I could learn to love His way. It's what I needed to do to go on.

God is the greatest teacher of all to show us how to love unconditionally. Live, learn, and trust God!!

It's the only way to have a good marriage!

FINAL DREAM

April 7, 2014, I was dreaming *I saw myself buying plain white T-shirts that were nice and neatly folded. I was bringing out one at a time. Then I saw that I collected an arm full of nice and neatly folded white T-shirts. I asked the Lord, "What do you want me to do with this?". The Lord said "He's saved".*

Then Chase woke me up. I said, "Why did you wake me up? I was talking to Jesus!". Chase asked, "You don't hear that alarm going off?". Get up. I'll take Sean to school". I went back to sleep. When Chase came back, he said, "Let's go to breakfast". I said, "Can you make it lunch instead? I'm sleepy". He got in the bed. I turned over and saw him sitting up with his arms folded. I asked, "What are you doing?". He said, I'm waiting for you to get up so we can go to breakfast". I said, "Okay! Fine!". I got up, got ready, and we went to breakfast. It was about 8:45am. We went to his favorite place, La Madeleine Cafe'. He always ordered hash browns, two eggs over easy, and a croissant with a cup of coffee. He always put a lot of sugar in his coffee.

As he put the sugar in his coffee. I just smiled, and shook my head. He said, "You know I like it with a lot of sugar". I said, "Yes, I know". I ordered eggs and bacon with coffee. We laughed while talking about people and the way they were sitting to eat. We were trying to guess what they were thinking about as they were eating. One man was sitting, just looking out the window at the traffic. Chase said the guy was thinking about if he would have just used the toilet before he got here, he would he be enjoying his coffee. I laughed so hard as we were talking about people, I couldn't eat my food. Then we started talking about his suspension from his jobs. He said, "I know I was wrong. Faith, you know how much I want to be a cop". I said, "I know, but you never follow rules. I think sometimes you want to do right, but you just don't. I don't think you should have been suspended so long from the sheriff office". Chase said, "I know. Maybe I can talk to my lieutenant. Maybe he will understand". I asked, "You mean manipulate your lieutenant?". Chase said, "You know what I mean. You're going to have a lot of money when I die". I said, "How much money? Your "a lot of money" is not my "a lot of money". You know I'm an Accountant". Chase said, "I know". I said, "Chase, you said that three times this morning. Are you going to die today?". Chase said, "I think so", then sighed. I said, "It's 12:15pm. I had a great time this morning, but let's go". I started thinking about all the years we've been together. The good and the bad, but mostly the good. That morning was so good that I didn't want to leave. The laughter reminded me like the beginning of our relationship. I know now that Chase gave me all he had to give. The only love he's known was mostly stuff. That's how he knew to show love. If he would've just listened, and watched me, he would have known that wasn't my kind of love. If I could go back to the beginning, maybe I would have shown him differently. I would have given him more affection. I think Chase would've still wanted more stuff. All I can say about Chase now is his good outweighs his bad. We picked up Sean early that day. Before going inside the school, Chase said, "When I die, don't move. Stay in the house.

It'll be paid off. Don't get a hysterectomy". I said, "Why? You going to die? I want your baby, not anyone else". He said, "I know, but I'd want to be here too. You always wanted your own baby". I said, "I got Sean, and that's all I need". We got Sean, and went home. About 3:15pm, Chase said, "I've got to go". He went to start his motorcycle. He came back in the hugged me with so much compassion and love. He said, "I love you. Fix me some hot dogs and chili for dinner". I walked to the door, and watched him get on the motorcycle. As I waited for him to pull off, I thought to myself, "I never watch him ride out". He waived, I waived, and I went back into the house. I knew at that moment he was not coming back.

PROPHET SEAN MYCAEL HAD A VISION

In the last days, God says, I will pour out my Spirit on all people. Your sons and daughters will prophesy, your young men will see visions, your old men will dream dreams. Act 2:17

About 7:15 pm, my Aunt Jo called and said, "Chase has been in an accident. You need to come over here". I said, "Is he dead?". She was quiet. I said, "I'm on my way". I called for Sean, and said to him, "Let's go to Mama Jo's house". We got in the car, and about three miles from Mama Jo's house, Sean took his seat belt off and came up to me. He said "Mama, daddy's not going to make it this time. I see his leg, Sean pointed, over there, and I see blood everywhere. He's not going to make it this time. Mama, are you going to be, okay?". I said, "Are you going to be, okay?". He said, "Yes". Sean sat back down, and put his seat belt on. I didn't understand Why God would give that vision to a six-year-old child. I always knew Sean was a gift from God. God had just revealed how gifted he is. When we got to the street where Mama Jo lives, the ambulance was leaving going the opposite direction going to hospital with Chase's body. I spoke quickly to my aunt and called Chase's mom. I told her Chase was in an accident and to meet me at the Mid-City Hospital. When Sean and I got to the hospital, my cousin was there. He had witnessed what had happened to Chase. He said there was blood everywhere, and his leg was cut off. The same thing Sean had said before we got to Mama Jo's house. The nurses had to give my cousin something to calm him down.

Most of my family was there. Some sheriff deputies were there, and also some postal workers. I spoke with the nurse that was over Chase's body remains. She said, "I can't let you see him". I walked away, then saw my ministers. They asked if they could see the body. I said, "The nurse said no one can see the body. I know you want to pray over him, but I know his time is up. Everything happens for a reason". God wouldn't let me see him. God didn't want me to lay hands on him. God told me his time was up. The waiting room was full. I described Chase's mother to the nurse. I asked the nurses not to tell his mother. I would tell her. Later, Chase's mother came in, but the nurse I told not to tell his mother, told her he had died. I was glad her aunt was with her at the time. I couldn't help her, nor would she let me.

PEACE OF GOD

And the peace of God, which surpasses all understanding, will guard your hearts and your minds in Christ Jesus. Phil. 4:7 9(NIV)

I know everything I've been through is for His purpose and His Glory. When we're going through it, it's natural to question God. I know all my life, I asked God, "Why does this have to happen to me. Lord? Can't you get me something else some other kind of way? The way I know I can handle? Lord, show me how to get through this with my husband. I know you should come first. You said I should honor my husband the way Sarah honored Abraham, like a master. Oh, Lord gives me what I need to go on. Show me what You called me to be. Keep me focused on the purpose in this race at this moment, and this place in my life. I'm feeling something I've never felt in my forty-four years of living. I don't understand this feeling I'm feeling. It feels like joy and comfort. I can't cry, I can't feel sad or unhappy. I feel calm. I want to help everyone that is hurting from my husband's death. I realize Chase's goods outweighed his bad. God, You gave me the peace that passes all understanding. I whole-heartedly loved my husband. I know he loved You, Lord. You told me the morning he died, that he was saved. Lord, I thank you for this peace. I know all is well! I know

You have more for me. I should finish this race. I'll go wherever you want me to go. I'll stay wherever you want me to stay. You said You will never leave me nor forsake me. If You are with me. I know now when it is something bad, it's happening for my good. You know what is best for me.

April 7, 2014, Chase was pronounced dead. April is the fourth month of the year. The number four is a new beginning. The number seven is the end of something. The funeral was on Tuesday, April 15th, tax-day. I knew some wouldn't able to make the funeral. When I got to the church. I saw so many sheriff cars and postal trucks. When I walked in the foyer of the church with Chase daughters, I looked around, and saw men on the floor, and in the corners crying. I walked through the church.

On one side, was sheriff and postal workers. On the other side was all family, mostly in the middle of a church. In the high rise of the church were Navy people, people he delivered mail to, and motorcycle riders. The church held about 3,000 people. The church was full. I couldn't believe all these people were there. Chase said he had a lot of "boys". I didn't know he had that many. As I was walking down the aisle, I heard a woman say, "Why she's not crying? I know she didn't love Chase". I took a guess that it was the women he was cheating on me with. It was a very nice service. We went to the cemetery. Because he was in the Navy, the wife gets a flag. I asked one of the men that were folding it to give it to his mother, so he did as I asked. After the burial, the Commanding Officer was mad that the officer gave the flag to Chase's mother. He told the officer he had to give it to his wife. I said, "No, I told him I wanted it to go to Chase's mother". They folded another one and gave it to me. I thanked them.

I spoke previously about my cousin Sheba who I went to church with on New Year's Eve, and prayed about our marriages. Four days after Chase died, Sheba's husband was found dead in his apartment. God will move things out of the way to get you in a place He needs you to be. It was April 7th when Chase died, and April 11th when Sheba's husband died. Biblical number 7 and number 11 means an Ending. The numbers 8 and 12 means new beginning. Sheba and I was about to begin a new beginning with our Lord.

The day after Chase was buried, I was sitting in my bed. I heard God say, "It was Chase's ending, and your new beginning". I asked God, "What should I do now?". God said, "Write the book, and open your shoe store". I said, "God, you know I'm not a writer". He didn't answer. I remember at that moment about Moses when he thought about his imperfections, but God worked it all out. I began writing this book a year later. I was now understanding why God told me to write this book. As I'm writing the book, it revealed something inside of me that I buried deep in me. The book was a part of my cleaning process. I needed this cleaning so bad. Writing this book, took me back to the beginning of my pain as a little girl. God has better for me, and I got to get myself together for my next adventure with Him. Another nurse asked if she could speak to me and his mother in a closed room. She explained to us why we couldn't see his body. She said, in a nice way, it was very damaged. As she was talking, one of Chase's deputy friends came through the door. He was very upset. He grabbed me, and hugged me as he cried. I knew he loved Chase like a brother. I asked his friend that was with him to help him. I couldn't help him at the time.

The love I looked for all my life I always had it.

Love, with no conditions. Agape love is the love God has for His children.

The new commend. I give you; Love one another. As I have loved you, so you must love one another. By this all men will know that you are my disciples, if you love one another. John 13:34-35

God sometimes puts us through things in order for us to grow into what He made us to be. Testing is one way we grow. We never know how long we'll be tested. God doesn't think like us or do what we do. "For my thoughts are not your thoughts, neither are your ways my ways, declared the Lord." Isaiah 55:8. We, as humans, have been trained to order "conditions" in a relationship. Love comes with no conditions. It's hard for most of us. In many new relationships, there are conditions. "If you love me, you'll give me money, or you'll make love to me". We are all born sinners. I guess we are born with conditions for love. Once we are born again, after renewing our minds (Rom12:2), we will see how to love unconditionally.

When I was young, I would sing love songs, and hope I would find the man who would give me the kind of love I needed and wanted. I grew up, and found the only love I needed and could ever want is the love of God. God shaped me and made me the woman I am now. He loved me like no one else could ever love. His love is unconditional.

I did not know what love was, I just knew it was good. Through my marriage, God has taught me how to love His way; unconditional. I learned that no matter what wrong has been done to me, I must forgive and keep on loving them. It's a very hard thing to do, especially when it's hard to love someone. The one's you love seems to be the one to hurt you the most. Being hurt so much as a little girl, I stopped showing people what could hurt me. I did cry, then, when I was hurting physically, mentally or emotionally. Now at forty-six years old, I can't cry. I practiced so long trying to cry, but I can't. In my marriage, my husband would hurt me to see if I would cry. I remember him saying, "Nothing hurts you". I told him I hurt a lot, but I don't show it by crying. The only time I cry is when I can feel God's presence. I can't speak or make a sound. I just want to die and be where God is all the time. I can't wait to get to Heaven. I want everyone, everywhere, to see what I see with God. There is nothing like it. I ask God to take me with Him. God tells me I'm selfish. He said, "I have work for you to do here". I must help others see what I see. I have to stay here for a little longer to help others accept Jesus.

Vera was a big part of my pain. I'd get compliments. My mother would belittle me so much, I couldn't receive anything good about myself. Chase would ask me why I change the subject when he says something good about me. He told me that I was a beautiful person inside and out, and when people tell me about my goodness, I should accept it. I was always looking for Vera's approval in my life. I thought I needed her acceptance. I needed her to say that no matter what I look like, I'm still her daughter, and possibly say she loved me. I didn't know that my mother's love was such a big factor in my life. My relationship with Vera is much better now. I'm willing to try harder to make it work. I don't want to pass this on to my son. I'm always telling him I love him. I'm always showing him unconditional love. He's very important to me. God gave him to me for His purpose. I have to teach him how to love people God's way. My grandmother showed me the love I needed and wanted while she was here on earth. God has always given me unconditional love. I'll always try to show my son unconditional love. Sean means the world to me. I will try to show love, because that is who God is, and wants us all to do.

This is my prayer the race I'm running with endurance: "I need You God to continually walk with me and guide me to the places You have for me to go in order to complete my assignments here on earth for You. Lord, help me with my sins of disrespect, and pride. I have the faith that You will never leave me. I Love You, Lord my God!!

In Jesus Name, Amen

www.ingramcontent.com/pod-product-compliance
Lightning Source LLC
LaVergne TN
LVHW050023080526
838202LV00069B/6895